ENGLISH

Teachers' Book

TEACHING SESSIONS FOR THE LITERACY HOUR

Contents

Introduction	General introduction	4
	Course components	5
	Approach and structure	6
	Planning with *Password English*	8
	How to use the course	11
WORD		
Spelling	Spelling strategies	14
	Sounds	20
	Verb spellings	24
	Word endings	28
	Compound words	32
	Spelling revision	34
Vocabulary	Dictionaries	40
	Word puzzles	44
	New words	50
	Transforming words	54
SENTENCE		
Grammar	Parts of speech	60
	Verbs	64
	Adverbs	72
	Adjectives	76
	Sentences	82
	Grammar revision	88
Punctuation	Commas in sentences	92
	Apostrophes	96
	Punctuation marks	98

TEXT		
Fiction	Authors	102
	Playscripts	108
	Characters	114
	Structure and sequence	120
	Settings	128
	Issues	136
	Stories from other cultures	144
Poetry	Common themes in poetry	150
	Classic and modern poetry	156
	Poetry: range of forms	162
Non-fiction	Newspapers	170
	Instructions	178
	Using ICT	182
	Presentation of information	186
	Information books	194
	Persuasive writing	200
	Discursive writing	206
TEACHERS' NOTES	Teaching and learning literacy	214
	The literacy hour	216
	Range of text types	218
	ICT and literacy	220
Coverage charts	NLS: scope and sequence charts	224
	Curriculum links	228
Assessment	General notes	234
	Charts	238
Simmering activities	Word level	244
	Sentence level	248
	Text level	252

General introduction

What is *Password English*?

Password English is a new English course with a refreshing and flexible approach to teaching literacy skills. It matches the approach of the National Literacy Strategy and offers thorough coverage of NLS objectives for word, sentence and text-level work (see chart on pages 224-227).

Password English delivers the requirements of the National Curriculum for English (England and Wales, 1995), the Scottish Guidelines on English Language 5-14 (1991), and the Northern Ireland Curriculum for English (1996) (see charts on pages 228-233).

How does it work?

The course is organised into skills-based sessions that have a straightforward three-step structure:

- **Teaching:** whole-class teaching of the skills to be covered in the session, using the *Teachers' Book*, *Big Book* and *Anthology*.

- **Developing:** independent differentiated group work to develop these skills, using activities in the *Textbook*, texts in the *Anthology*, and photocopiable activity sheets in the *Differentiated Practice* book.

- **Reflecting:** plenary session to review, reflect, consolidate and share work.

In addition, the *Homework* photocopiable sheets offer further support, practice and extension of key skills.

In this way, *Password English* offers an exceptionally flexible approach that mirrors the structure of the literacy hour, but at the same time can be adapted to suit particular needs.

Course components

Teachers' Book A structured, easy-to-use guide for direct teaching and differentiated group work, plus background information for teachers.

Big Book  A range of stimulating texts, including fiction, poetry and non-fiction, designed to be used with the whole class.

Textbook Full-colour activities to practise and support key skills, designed for independent group work.

Anthology A wide range of fiction, poetry and non-fiction for use with groups or the whole class.

Differentiated Practice  A collection of photocopiable activities to support, reinforce and extend key skills, designed for independent group work.

Homework  Extra photocopiable activities to reinforce and develop skills, designed to be tackled at home.

Approach and structure

General approach and rationale

Password English reflects the following key ideas about the teaching and learning of literacy:

- Direct and systematic instruction has a vital role to play in children's acquisition of literacy skills and understanding. The *Password English Teachers' Book* is the key resource, providing detailed, practical guidance on whole-class and group teaching strategies for each session.

- Balancing this direct instruction, children need opportunities to engage in sharply focused and challenging literacy activities. A range of differentiated activities of this kind are suggested in the *Teachers' Book* and provided directly in the *Textbook* and photocopiable materials.

- Reading and writing are closely related in the development of literacy. *Password English* sessions are designed so that reading and writing activities feed into and support one another.

- Work on different aspects of literacy needs to be balanced and integrated. *Password English* covers and interrelates work at word, sentence and text levels.

- Children should experience a wide range of fiction, poetry and non-fiction. A variety of genres and text types are included at each stage of *Password English*.

- Broader aspects of literacy learning are integrated throughout, including activities using speaking and listening and ICT (Information and Communications Technology).

In this way, *Password English* reflects both the approach and the coverage of the National Literacy Strategy.

Structure of stages

Password English for juniors is divided into year group stages 3, 4, 5 and 6, each fulfilling the needs of the corresponding primary school year (in Scotland, P4, 5, 6, 7). Each stage consists of 100 sessions, which are grouped into units. Each session is focused on a particular skill and is designed to last about an hour.

Structure of units

Each *Password English* unit has a sharp and sustained focus on the development of a particular literacy skill or area of understanding. Some units consist of just one session. Others consist of a series of between two and four linked sessions. Wherever possible, work on these units should be continuous (across a sequence of literacy hours).

Structure of sessions

All *Password English* sessions are organised in three parts, corresponding to the organisational and teaching approaches to be used in the implementation of the literacy hour:
- teaching
- developing
- reflecting.

A more detailed explanation of this approach is given on pages 11-13. The session structure corresponds to the requirements of the literacy hour, and is designed to fit flexibly with teachers' planning to ensure sufficient coverage of word, sentence and text-level objectives.

Each session contains a clear cross-reference to the National Literacy Strategy framework for teaching. For example:
- T1/W7 – term 1, word level, point 7
- T2/S2 – term 2, sentence level, point 2
- T3/T11 – term 3, text level, point 11

Planning with *Password English*

Flexibility

The 100 sessions in each stage of *Password English* are designed so that you can incorporate them flexibly into literacy hours and other planning frameworks, according to your school's schemes of work for English.

Planning a literacy hour

Using *Password English* in this context will involve the same planning steps and considerations as for any literacy hour.

1. Identify the aims and content of the literacy hour, referring to the National Literacy Strategy framework of objectives (or your school's scheme of work). Note that at Key Stage 2, each literacy hour should include a combination of work at text, word and/or sentence levels. This will need to be incorporated into your short-term planning.

2. Select the *Password English* unit that relates to these objectives. Information at the top of each session shows whether the main focus of the session is on word, sentence or text-level work. Many sessions provide linked work at more than one level.

3. Gather or prepare any resources.

4. Decide which groups will take part in which activities and on which groups you will focus your support. (Remember that a range of activities is provided, from which you could select two or three, or use them all. You might also want each group to take part in more than one of the activities suggested in the session.)

Planning a sequence of literacy hours

Literacy hours, like all teaching sessions, need to be planned not singly but in sequences, informed by the school's medium and long-term scheme of work and objectives. Planning for a week of literacy hours at a time is a useful strategy here. It will involve the following tasks:

1. Deciding on the objectives to be covered during the week, and what your teaching focus will be on each day. For example, you could:

- use the *Password English* units with more than one session as the basis for a week's work; these provide a substantial amount of material, yet each session has it own focus

- draw together *Password English* units that focus on the same area of word or sentence-level work, e.g. spelling or punctuation

- make links between text and word and/or sentence-level work, e.g. work on a poetry unit could feed into and support work on vocabulary or a particular part of speech.

2. Planning a range of activities to enable each group to engage in the appropriate activities. For example, there may be some activities that you want all groups to complete, and some activities that you want the children to complete individually.

3. Deciding how to organise your own time so that each group receives its share of intensive support.

4. Deciding how to link the teaching from day to day. For instance, you could:

- consolidate or extend the children's understanding by revisiting an aspect of literacy introduced in an earlier session (many *Password English* sessions contain a substantial amount of material, and you may well feel this is advisable)
- organise the week's work to highlight the links between literacy focuses, e.g. from exploring rhyme schemes in poems to looking at spelling patterns
- organise the week's work so that there are opportunities to draw it together in the final sessions (*Password English* units that consist of more than one session are devised with this structure).

Other planning approaches

Password English can also be used in planning based on blocked and continuing units of work. For example, units with several sessions focused on reading and writing particular kinds of texts could be the basis for planning blocked units of work. Units on aspects of spelling, vocabulary, grammar and punctuation could be incorporated into continuing work.

Coverage and planning

Password English is designed as a core resource that covers the key skills. For example, key spelling skills and concepts are covered, but these will still need to be practised and consolidated throughout the year using a suitable spelling resource. Key reading skills are covered, but children will benefit from a structured, graded reading programme.

Password English is a structured and accessible tool for teaching and learning that will complement your existing resources and form the heart of your literacy teaching programme.

How to use the course

Unit heading: specifies the key literacy skill covered

Focus: specifies main focus of session; reference to NLS framework

Session number: the number of sessions in each unit

Learning objectives: specific and achievable aims for the session

Cross-references: links to *Password English* components and other resources

---

Parts of speech

2/2

Focus
Sentence level
Grammar: nouns, pronouns, verbs, adjectives
T1, 2, 3revision

Learning objectives
- to consolidate knowledge of basic parts of speech
- to recognise more complex uses of nouns and adjectives

TEACHING: *whole-class introduction*   *Resources*

- Remind the children about the basic parts of speech they revised in the previous session: nouns, pronouns, verbs and adjectives.

- Split the class into groups of three. Each group should invent a sentence containing a noun, verb and adjective. Listen to, and comment on, each sentence.

- **Shared text:** read the extract from *How the Whale Became and Other Stories* in the Big Book. Focus on nouns: *birds, feathers, feet*. The children should recognise these as 'straightforward' nouns as they have defined them: *the name of a person, place or thing*. Then look at the word *darkness*. Explain that this is a noun, even though it is not a person, place or really a 'thing'. You cannot hold it, pick it up or do anything with it: it is an *abstract noun*. Discuss other examples, e.g. *happiness, sadness, other feelings, ideas*, etc.   Big Book page 7

- Look at the expression *the new country* at the end of the first paragraph. The children should recognise *new* as a 'straightforward' adjective, placed before the noun. Then look at the first sentence: *The birds grew thin.* Ask the children which word is the adjective (*thin*) and stress that adjectives do not always have to be in front of the noun. Ask them to think of other examples, e.g. *The girl was tall; The dog was smelly; The car was so clean it shone.*

Parts of speech

DEVELOPING: *group activities*   *Resources*

- Write five to ten simple sentences using adjectives that are not in front of the noun. e.g. *The cat was black. The class is noisy.*✶

- Follow on from the whole-class session by listing as many abstract nouns as possible. Collect them on to a poster for display.✶✶   Dictionary / ICT

- Using a favourite reading book or other text, find examples of nouns and/or adjectives used in the way discussed with the whole class. Be ready to share examples.✶✶   Reading books

- Identify nouns, pronouns, verbs and adjectives in a text extract, including abstract nouns and adjectives that are remote from the nouns they are describing.✶✶   Textbook page 18

- Write the opening of a story called *Nigel and the Noun Factory*, where Nigel has to sort out abstract nouns, proper nouns and common nouns. Include examples of each kind of noun. Use a dictionary for help.✶✶✶   Dictionary

REFLECTING: *plenary*

- Share the simple sentences containing adjectives and write more to add to the list.

- Share and discuss examples of nouns and adjectives found in reading books. Which examples does the class like best?

ASSESSMENT
- Use knowledge of basic parts of speech confidently and accurately.
- Recognise and use more complex forms of nouns and adjectives.

TEACHING Suggestions for whole-class introduction of key skills

DEVELOPING A range of carefully differentiated group activities

REFLECTING Opportunities to share, review, reflect and consolidate work

Assessment Points to assess progress, linked to learning objectives

TEACHING: whole-class introduction	Under this heading you will find detailed, step-by-step guidance on introducing and teaching the aspect of literacy covered in the session. The emphasis is on direct teaching in the context of shared reading and writing activities. A number of teaching strategies recur, including demonstration, explanation modelling and questioning. In most cases, work in this whole-class phase is based on a shared text. This might be a page from the *Password English Big Book* or *Anthology*, from another big book in your classroom, or a short text to be written on the board or chart. When sharing a text, it is important to ensure that all the children can see it clearly. Many sessions involve drawing attention to particular words or phrases, e.g. by circling.
DEVELOPING: group activities	Under this heading, you will find a range of three to five activities for groups of children. All these activities are directly related to the objectives in the teaching phase, and are designed to enable children to develop their skills and understanding. There are opportunities for practice and consolidation; for approaching the topic in different ways; and for exploring the topic in relation to specific texts and contexts. The majority of activities are designed so that they can be completed within approximately 20 minutes allotted to group work within the structure of the literacy hour. If children do not complete an activity, perhaps because it proves more challenging than expected or because they find a way of expanding it, the work can be taken over into the next literacy hour. Some activities are identified as offering opportunities for more extended work, especially

reading and/or writing longer texts. This work can be pursued over a number of literacy hours or outside this context.

The ICT logo indicates activities that could use ICT opportunities, although these could be developed and extended where appropriate.

The activities are designed for independent group work. Following the input from the teaching phase, children should be able to work on them with little direct teacher intervention or support. However, each activity also offers an opportunity for you to work intensively with the group, guiding and supporting its work. You will also need to consider requirements for guided reading, using reading material from outside the course.

To help you match these activities to the needs of different groups of children, they are listed in order of challenge, starting with the least demanding. They are indicated by the following symbols:
◆ lower ability for age group
◆◆ mid ability for age group
◆◆◆ high ability for age group.

Although the activities have been devised with collaborative group work in mind, most can be readily adapted for pair or individual work.

REFLECTING: plenary
Each session ends with a whole-class plenary. Guidance here suggests strategies for sharing, presenting and discussing work, reflecting and raising questions, consolidating the teaching points, and identifying ways of taking the work forward.

Spelling strategies

Focus
Word level
Spelling: improving
spelling
T1/general; T1, 2, 3/W4

Learning objectives
- to revise and consolidate knowledge of spelling strategies
- to improve awareness of spelling rules

TEACHING: *whole-class introduction*

Resources

- **Shared text:** use the shared text to introduce or remind the children of the *look, say, cover, write, check* strategy: each child *looks* at the word, *says* it aloud, *covers* it up, *writes* it down and then *checks* for accuracy.

  Shared text

- Introduce the game of Spelling Champions. Split the children into mixed-ability groups or 'teams'. Write up a short list of challenging words; each team must use *look, say, cover, write, check* when writing the word. Find the champions, using either:
  - a points system: a team scores one point for each correct spelling; the first team to score 10 points is the champion
  - a 'knockout' system: teams are knocked out if they spell a word incorrectly; the last remaining team is the champion.

- Explain that there are some important spelling rules to help them with tricky words: give the example of *i before e except after c*. Ask them to suggest other spelling rules they know.

- Remind the children of the value and purpose of word banks and spelling logs. Discuss examples of banks or logs that they have used in the past, e.g. whole-class logs, individual word banks, other class collections of words.

Spelling strategies

Resources

DEVELOPING: *group activities*

- Design and produce an attractive poster as a reminder of *look, say, cover, write, check.*◆

- As a group, share three ways of remembering difficult spellings. Think of two or three tricky words and invent ways of remembering them.◆

- Find new examples to illustrate a range of common spelling rules.◆◆

| Practice PCM 1 |

- As a group, plan the design for a class word bank. Think about how it might be used, what words might be included and where it could be stored in the classroom.◆◆

- Devise a game to find out the best speller in the group using the approach outlined for the earlier Spelling Champions game.◆◆◆

REFLECTING: *plenary*

- Play one of the games devised by the groups to find the overall class spelling champion.

- Compile a class list of spelling rules and strategies used in this session. What spelling rules can the children remember? Which ones do they use most often?

Homework

- Identify incorrect spellings and write them correctly.◆◆

| Homework PCM 1 |

ASSESSMENT
- Use a range of spelling strategies.
- Show awareness of spelling rules and strategies for improving spelling.

Spelling strategies

2/3

Focus
Word level
Spelling: visual spelling skills
T1, 2, 3/W3; T3/W5

Learning objectives
- to develop visual skills in spelling
- to identify common letter strings at the beginning, middle and end of words

Resources

TEACHING: *whole-class introduction*

- **Shared text:** use the shared text to introduce the idea of using the *look* of words to help with spelling. After the text has been read, ask the children to suggest which words might be most difficult to spell. Examine these words together, for example:
  - look for letter strings that could help, e.g. remembering *ough* in *brought*
  - break the word into smaller parts, e.g. *Wed-nes-day*
  - identify letter strings that often come at the beginning of words, e.g. *wo: worship, won*
  - identify letter strings that often come at the end of words, e.g. *ss: goodness, hiss*

  Shared text

- Ask the children to suggest words they find difficult to spell. Do they use the way a word *looks* to help remember the correct spelling? If necessary, prompt a discussion about the following ideas:
  - looking for common letter strings (as practised with the shared text)
  - does it look right e.g. is it the right shape, length, etc?

- Read out this list of words and ask the children to write them correctly, using the ideas already discussed:
  - began
  - brought
  - found
  - know
  - stopped
  - thought
  - heard
  - walking
  - write

  If necessary, repeat this test at the end of the session to assess progress.

Spelling strategies

DEVELOPING: *group activities*

- Write a letter to the shop manager, telling him of his spelling mistakes.◆

- Choose two pages from the Anthology (or a favourite reading book) and conduct a survey to find out the most common letter strings. Present the results in a simple chart or table.◆◆

- Examine a list of spelling strategies and design a classroom poster as a reminder of the points.◆◆

- With a partner, write a list of five to ten words that are difficult to spell. Check the spellings using the ideas discussed with the whole class (e.g. *does it look right?*), then check using a dictionary.◆◆

- Invent a fair spelling test for another group which tests their ability to spell words with more than two syllables.◆◆◆

REFLECTING: *plenary*

- If necessary, repeat the spelling test from the beginning of the session to assess how much progress has been made.

- Discuss the posters and establish whether each of them is clear and approved of by the class as a whole.

Homework
- Think up ways to remember tricky spellings.◆◆

Resources

Practice PCM 2

Anthology

Reading book

Textbook page 3

ICT
Dictionary

Homework PCM 2

ASSESSMENT
- Apply visual and observational skills to spelling.
- Identify and use common letter strings.

Spelling strategies

3/3

Focus
Word level
Spelling: patterns
T1, 2, 3/W3; T2/W6; T3/W7

Learning objectives
- to spell by analogy with other words
- to recognise patterns in words and apply them to their own spelling

TEACHING: *whole-class introduction*

Resources

- **Shared text:** use the shared text to explore and identify words with similar patterns, e.g. letter strings (*enough, bought*), common roots (*invent, prevent*), common endings (*light, fright*), and so on. Write up some examples.

  Shared text

- Use this to stimulate discussion of spelling patterns:
  - **Families:** discuss how words sometimes come in families: e.g. *medicine, medical, medication; science, scientist, scientific*. Write up a well-known word (e.g. *help, know*) and encourage the children to suggest as many words as possible that are members of the same word family (e.g. *helper, helpful, helping*).
  - **Patterns:** encourage the children to think of examples of words that share letter strings, even if they sound different e.g. *rough, cough, through; ball, shall; height, weight*.
  - **Endings:** show how some words have common endings: e.g. *-tion: section, fiction; -ight: right, might, light; -ough: tough, rough*.
  - **Roots:** explore and discuss words with common roots and suggest examples, e.g. *phone, telephone, microphone; advent, invent, prevent*.

- Discuss little words in big words as another useful spelling idea, e.g. how many words are there in *carpenter*? (*car, carp, pen, enter*)

Spelling strategies

DEVELOPING: *group activities*

- Match the words that belong to the same word family, then write new lists.◆

- Spelling challenge: groups could choose from the following activities, or all work on the same one, using their collective knowledge, word banks, dictionaries, reading books, etc. Prepare to present the results to the rest of the class.◆◆
  - letter string challenge: find as many words as possible that have a chosen letter string, e.g. *-ough*
  - word endings challenge: as above, but find as many words as possible that have a chosen ending, e.g. *-ight*
  - roots challenge: as above, but find a range of words that have common roots, e.g. *vent*.

- Write sentences using some or all of the words discussed.◆◆◆

REFLECTING: *plenary*

- Present the results from the spelling challenge activities. Which challenge was the most difficult? Why?

- Share the sentences written and discuss the spelling points covered in the session. Are they clear?

Homework

- Find little words inside long place names.◆◆

Resources

Practice PCM 3

Dictionaries

Reading books

Homework PCM 3

ASSESSMENT
- Use various patterns as clues to show understanding of the idea of spelling by analogy.
- Recognise patterns in words and apply knowledge of them.

Sounds

Focus
Word level
Spelling: homophones
T1/W6

Learning objectives
- to recognise that the same sound can be represented by different letter strings
- to understand and use the term *homophone*

TEACHING: *whole-class introduction*

Resources

- **Shared text:** use the shared text to focus on the idea of word sounds. If possible, locate and discuss simple homophones, e.g. *to, two, too; there, their.*

  Shared text

- Recap previous work on homophones (words that sound the same but are spelt differently) from Stage 3. Write up one word from a homophone pair (e.g. *week, hair, sea, fir, pair*) and ask the children to say and spell the other word in the pair (*weak, hare, see, fur, pear*).

- Ask the children to suggest other examples of homophone pairs. Write them on the board, or ask volunteers to write them. Ensure the children understand the meaning of each word.

- Use an example (e.g. *week/weak*) to draw out the more general point that some vowel sounds (especially long vowel sounds) can be spelt in different ways.

- Use words from the list and other examples to build up a list of the different ways of spelling the long vowel sounds for:
  - *a* (e.g. as in *pay, wait, great, late, weight*)
  - *e* (e.g. as in *feet, meat, piece*).

  This activity could be extended to cover other common long vowel sounds, as in *moon* and *coat*.

Sounds

DEVELOPING: *group activities*

- Choose from the homophone groups *to/too/two* and *there/their* to fill gaps in sentences. Write more sentences using these words. ◆

- Select from a homophone pair the word that makes sense in a sentence. Write new sentences. ◆◆

- Compile lists of words showing the different ways in which the long *a* sound can be spelt. ◆◆

- As a group, devise a spelling test for the class focused on homophones and/or on different ways of spelling long vowel sounds. The children could present the test as a list of words or, more challenging and more interesting, as a dictation text. ◆◆◆

- Challenge the children to find less usual homophone pairs (e.g. *dough/doe*) and homophone trios (e.g. *rain/reign/rein, so/sow/sew, to/two/too, pair/pear/pare*). ◆◆◆

Resources

Practice PCM 4

Practice PCM 5

Textbook page 4

ICT

REFLECTING: *plenary*

- Share unusual and interesting homophone pairs and trios they have found.

- Carry out and mark the spelling test. Are any words particularly tricky? Why?

Homework

- Complete sentences by using the correct homophone from a pair. ◆◆

Homework PCM 4

ASSESSMENT
- Understand and use the term *homophone*.
- Recognise and use a range of homophones.

Sounds

2/2

Focus
Word level
Spelling: homographs
T3/W6

Learning objectives
- to recognise that the same letter string can represent different sounds
- to understand and use the term *homograph*

TEACHING: *whole-class introduction*

Resources

- **Shared text:** read the Big Book page, perhaps with volunteers taking a sentence each. Homographs are words with the same spelling but different sounds, in this case *wind, tear, row, bow, read, lead* and *close*.

Big Book page 2

- If the children hesitate over or misread one of the homographs, prompt them to identify the two possible sounds and select the right one for this text. If not, ask them what they notice about each word. How else can it be pronounced? What does it mean if they pronounce it like that? How did they know how to say it?

- Shared writing: confirm the different meanings and pronunciations of the homographs by writing sentences in which each is used in its other sense. Read these sentences out loud.

- Draw out from these examples the more general idea that the same letter string can be pronounced in different ways. Point out that this is the opposite of the case explored in the previous session. Explain and illustrate this with examples, e.g. for *-ea* (as in *meat, bread, great*); *-oth* (as in *moth, both, brother*); *-ose* (as in *rose, lose, dose*); *-ear* (as in *fear, pear*); *-ow* (*cow, blow*); and if you wish the notorious *-ough* (*bough, cough*).

Sounds

DEVELOPING: *group activities*

- Use picture clues to investigate and write pairs of words in which the same letter string has two different sounds.◆

- Sort words with the same letter strings into sets according to the sound they make (focusing on -*ea* words and -*ou* words).◆◆

- Think of other words with the letter strings discussed in the whole-class session. Compile lists and sort them according to sound.◆◆

- Compile a list of word pairs for classroom display, by writing down words in which the same letter string has a different sound, e.g. *cough/bough*. Use a dictionary for reference if necessary and illustrate the words chosen.◆◆

- As a group, devise a spelling test for the class focused on the different sounds that the same letter string can represent. The children could present the test as a list of words or, more challenging and more interesting, as a dictation text.◆◆◆

Resources

Practice PCM 6

Practice PCM 7

 ICT

Dictionary

REFLECTING: *plenary*

- Share interesting or unusual spellings and sounds they have found.

- Carry out and mark the spelling test; are any words particularly tricky? Why?

ASSESSMENT
- Understand and use the term *homograph*.
- Recognise and use a range of homographs.

Verb spellings

1/2

Focus
Word level
Spelling: regular verb endings
T1/W7

Learning objectives
- to recognise spelling patterns related to verb endings *-s*, *-ing* and *-ed*
- to use these patterns accurately in writing

TEACHING: *whole-class introduction*

Resources

- Recap the idea that verbs take several different forms depending on their tense, e.g. write up a regular set such as *help, helps, helping, helped*. Highlight the endings and write up more examples, e.g. *walk, jump, play, rain*. Explain that in most cases these endings can simply be added to the root word.

- **Shared text:** show the Big Book page, and ask the children what they notice about the words *running, hopping* and *sitting*. Draw out the fact that the final consonant is doubled. Explain that *-ing* and *-ed* cannot always simply be added, and introduce the rule: verbs ending consonant-vowel-consonant – double the final consonant before adding *-ing* or *-ed*. Ask the children to suggest more examples.

  Big Book page 3

- Repeat this process with the words *sliding* and *shining*, introducing the rule: verbs ending with an *e* – drop this letter before adding *-ing* or *-ed*.
  NOTE: There are exceptions to these rules (e.g. *mix, shoe*), but they provide a good guide.

- Explain that the spelling rules for adding *-s* to verbs are the same as those for adding *-s* to make a noun plural, that is:
  - verbs ending in *consonant-y*, change *-y* to *-i* and add *-es* (*tidy/tidies* but *pay/pays*)
  - verbs ending in *-s, -sh, -ch, -tch* and *-x*: add *-es* (*miss/misses*)

Verb spellings

DEVELOPING: *group activities*

- Correct errors in a text where *-ing* and *-ed* have been added to verbs incorrectly.◆

- List words following the three patterns for adding *-ing* and *-ed*. Write a simple list poem based on verbs ending with *-ing*.◆◆

- Write an account of an activity yesterday or last weekend, paying special attention to the spelling of verbs ending in *-ed*.◆◆

- Write sentences describing what is going on now in the classroom, using verbs ending in *-s* and/or *-ing*.◆◆

- Compile a list of verbs and add *-ing* and *-ed* to each. These could be added to the class word bank. Use a dictionary for help if necessary.◆◆◆

REFLECTING: *plenary*

- Share writing from the group activities. Identify and discuss any *-ing* and *-ed* words that pose particular difficulties or that seem not to follow the rules (e.g. *carry/carrying; marry/marrying*).

- Set and give a brief *-s*, *-ing* and *-ed* spelling test, drawing on words from PCM 8.

Homework

- Write the correct spelling of verbs in sentences.◆◆

Resources

Practice PCM 8

Textbook page 5

ICT

Dictionary

Homework PCM 5

ASSESSMENT
- Recognise regular spelling patterns for verb endings.
- Use these patterns accurately in writing.

Verb spellings

2/2

Focus
Word level
Spelling: irregular verbs
T1/W8

Learning objectives
- to recognise the spelling of common irregular past-tense forms
- to use these forms accurately in writing

TEACHING: *whole-class introduction*

Resources

- **Shared text:** use the shared text to briefly recap work from the previous session on adding *-ed* to verbs to indicate that something happened in the past. Ask the children to identify regular past-tense verbs in the text.

  Shared text

- Ask the children to think about the word *sit*: can it be turned into the word *sitted*? What should the word be? Make clear that not all verbs follow the 'add *-ed*' pattern; instead there is a different, special spelling for particular words.

- Write up the sentence frames *I like to* _____. *Yesterday, I* _____. Complete them with common irregular verbs to show the shift from present to past tense, e.g. *I like to run. Yesterday, I ran all the way to school.* (See Textbook and photocopiable materials for other examples of irregular verbs.)

- Prompt the children to suggest and try out other verbs in this sentence frame. Draw their attention to recurring patterns, e.g. *find, wind/found, wound; grow, know/knew, blew.*

- *NOTE:* children's spelling of past-tense verbs may well be influenced by the non-standard forms with which they are familiar, e.g. *comed* for *came*, *growed* for *grew*. This will need to be handled sensitively.

Verb spellings

DEVELOPING: *group activities*

- Complete lists of irregular verbs in the present and past tenses.◆

- Rewrite instructions as a description of the activity, changing verbs from present to past tense.◆◆

- Use a list in the present tense (e.g. *write a thank you letter*) as the basis for writing a diary entry in the past tense (e.g. *I wrote a thank you letter*).◆◆

- Look back over recent pieces of writing to find and list irregular past-tense verbs. Which ones do they know how to spell? Which do they still need to learn? Write these out correctly, and learn, using the *look, say, cover, write, check* method.◆◆

- Compile a list of irregular past-tense spellings. Sort them and try to identify recurring patterns and families of words.◆◆◆

Resources

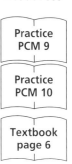

REFLECTING: *plenary*

- Set a test of irregular past tense spellings.

- Share and discuss the irregular verbs used in the group activities. What patterns have the children found? Which words are especially tricky? What helps us remember them?

Homework

- Write sentences to demonstrate understanding of irregular verb spellings.◆◆

Homework PCM 6

ASSESSMENT
- Recognise irregular spelling forms for past-tense verbs.
- Use these forms accurately in writing.

Word endings

Focus
Word level
Spelling: suffixes
T1/W9, T3/W9

Learning objectives
- to revise basic knowledge of suffixes
- to identify and use a range of new suffixes

TEACHING: *whole-class introduction*

Resources

- Remind the children that prefixes are added at the beginning of words and suffixes at the end. (Today's focus – suffixes!)

- **Shared text:** read the text from the Big Book. Re-read the text and ask the children to find examples of words with suffixes. Underline or highlight these examples.

Big Book page 4

- Discuss the construction of straightforward cases where root word and suffix are joined with no spelling complications, using word sums (e.g. *work + ing, proper + ly, danger + ous, safe + ty*).

- Discuss the examples where spelling modifications are needed. Stress these are familiar changes but care needs to be taken.
  – drop final *e*   (*cycle + ing = cycling*)
  – double final consonant   (*fit + ed = fitted*)
  – change *y* to *i*   (*carry + ed = carried*)

- The full list of words with suffixes in the Big Book text is as follows:
  – work**ing**   – proper**ly**   – cyc**ling**
  – fitt**ed**   – carr**ied**   – danger**ous**
  – help**ful**   – safe**ty**   – clear**ly**
  – atten**tion**   – expens**ive**
  – respons**ible** – sens**ible**.

Word endings

DEVELOPING: *group activities*

- Following on from the whole-class session, give the group 5-10 words with suffixes from the Big Book text and ask them to write sentences of their own using the words, to show that they understand the meaning of each one.◆

- Underline suffixes in a list of adjectives and choose from that list to complete a school report.◆◆

- Identify words with suffixes, write words as word sums, provide own examples with the same suffix, and form opposites by changing the suffix.◆◆

- List as many words as possible that end with *-ment* and *-ness*. Check all spellings in a dictionary and prepare to present them to the rest of the class.◆◆

- List as many words as possible that end with *-able* and *-ible*, *-tion* and *-sion*. Check all spellings in a dictionary and prepare to present them to the rest of the class.◆◆◆

REFLECTING: *plenary*

- Survey all the different suffixes encountered in the group activities (divide them on the board into those beginning with a vowel and those beginning with a consonant).

- Give the children a suffixes spelling test, drawing on words from the group activities.

Resources

ICT

Practice PCM 11

Textbook page 7

Dictionary

ASSESSMENT
- Identify and use a range of suffixes.
- Apply spelling rules accurately and use suffixes in writing.

Word endings

2/2

Focus
Word level
Spelling: building words
T2/W5, T3/W8

Learning objectives
- to investigate adding suffixes to words ending in -*f* and -*fe*
- to extend knowledge of suffixes in word building, related to spelling

TEACHING: *whole-class introduction*

Resources

- Ask the children to think of examples of words ending in -*f* and -*fe*, e.g. *brief, chief, life, leaf, half, thief, calf, knife*.

- Point out that most words ending in -*f* and -*fe* can just add suffixes as normal, e.g. *briefly, chiefly*. A few important exceptions change the *f* to *v*, e.g. *lively, halved, thieving*.

- When the children are confident with these spellings, move on to discuss adding other word endings.

- Look again at the Big Book text from the previous session. Ask the children to find the words that end with -*ful* (*helpful*) and -*ly* (*properly, clearly*).

  Big Book page 4

- Ask the children to think of other words ending in -*ful*. Establish that when *full* is used as a suffix it is always spelled -*ful*, e.g. *helpful, cheerful, harmful*. Invite further examples.

- Ask the children to think of other words ending in -*ly*. Why does *properly* have one *l* and *usually* have two? Think of (and spell) other examples, e.g. *really, actually, usefully, helpfully*.

- If time allows, extend the discussion to adding other suffixes and the spelling patterns involved, e.g. -*ive* (*expensive*), -*tion* (*attention*), -*ist* (*tourist*).

Word endings

DEVELOPING: *group activities*

- Write as many words as possible ending in *-ful* and *-ly*. Use a dictionary for help. ◆

- Use the words generated in the whole-class session to write a given number of sentences (to demonstrate that the meaning and spelling of each word is fully understood). ◆◆

- Write at least five words using these suffixes: *-ful, -ly, -ive, -tion, -ic, -ist*. Choose three words and write notes to explain how the meaning is changed by adding a suffix, e.g. *care – careful*. Use a dictionary for help if necessary. ◆◆

- Identify suffixes in a text, write some of them as word sums, then write a list of adjectives with suffixes. ◆◆

- Make a poster that will help everyone in the class remember spellings when adding suffixes to *-f* and *-fe* words. Include any exceptions and explain them clearly. ◆◆◆

Resources

Dictionary

Dictionary

Textbook pages 8-9

ICT

REFLECTING: *plenary*

- Discuss how the meaning and spelling of words is linked through suffixes.

- Share the poster about *-f* and *-fe* words and discuss how it could be improved.

ASSESSMENT
- Use suffixes correctly with words ending in *-f* and *-fe*.
- Recognise and understand the impact of word building and suffixes on the meaning of words.

Compound words

Focus
Word level
Spelling: compound words
T3/W11

Learning objectives
- to extend knowledge of compound words
- to investigate and use new compound words

TEACHING: *whole-class introduction*

Resources

- **Shared text:** use the shared text to remind the children of the work already done on compound words in Stage 3. Check that they understand the term and what it means, e.g. by providing a few examples and asking them to suggest others, identifying the two words of which they consist. Simple examples include *football, snowman, bedroom, goalpost*.

    Shared text

- Move on to illustrate and explain the idea of families of compound words; that is, sets of compound words that begin or end with the same word-part, e.g. *earache, eardrops, eardrum, earring; daylight, headlight, lamplight, firelight*.

- Work together to list other such families of words. *Back, over* and *eye* provide several possibilities for beginnings; *room, man*, and *board* for endings. Stress that identifying the two parts of the word can help when spelling the whole word.

- Extend the range by including words with more abstract meanings and with a structural function, e.g.: *everything, everyone; nothing, something, anything; outside, inside, beside; himself, herself*.

- Stress again how thinking of the parts of words helps spelling, including cases in which the sound of the word hides the fact that it is made up of two words, e.g. *cupboard, handbag, forehead, handkerchief*.

Compound words

DEVELOPING: *group activities*

- Continue the whole-class activity by compiling lists of families of compound words, using a dictionary.◆

- Find the word-part that will complete families of compound words (answers: *back, bed, book, day, eye, foot, over, out*). Invent new compound words.◆◆

- Invent, define and illustrate a range of new compound words.◆◆

- Find interesting and unusual compound words in the dictionary; think about the words of which they are made up and their meaning. Be ready to present the information to the rest of the class.◆◆

- Find the word that can go both before and after another word-part to make two compound words. (Answers: *bath, body, time, down, light, sight, book, side, head.*) Set similar puzzles for friends.◆◆◆

Resources

Dictionary

Dictionary

Dictionary

REFLECTING: *plenary*

- Share interesting compound words that have been found.

- Share and discuss compound words that they have invented. What do they mean? What words are they made up from? What other words could they invent?

Homework

- Match two halves of compound words.◆

ASSESSMENT
- Understand and use a range of compound words.
- Recognise how compound words can aid spelling.

Spelling revision

Focus
Word level
Spelling: double consonants
T1/W5

Learning objectives
- to spell two-syllable words containing double consonants
- to use such words effectively in writing

TEACHING: *whole-class introduction*

Resources

- Ask those children whose first names begin with a vowel to stand up. Ask if all the vowels are represented. Ask if anyone can remember the name describing all the other letters: *consonant*. Find out who has the most of either in their names.

- **Shared text:** use the shared text to identify any words with double consonants. Ask the volunteers to write each word on the board.

    Shared text

- Add the following pairs to the existing list on the board: *bitter-biter; dinner-diner; comma-coma; dotted-doted; ragged-raged.* Discuss the different sounds and meaning of each word and point out that single consonants have a long vowel before them (*diner*) and double consonants have a short vowel (*dinner*). Can the children think of any other examples?

- Double Consonant game: write up a list of double consonants: *bb, cc, dd, ff, gg,* etc. Go round the children (individuals, pairs or groups) in turn, asking for one word with that particular double consonant in it. If they are wrong, or cannot think of one, they are 'out'. Remember that some consonants are never doubled, e.g. *h, k, w, j*.

- Identify any unusual or unexpected words, e.g. *drizzle, trekking.*

Spelling revision

DEVELOPING: *group activities*

- Identify and correct spelling errors in a text involving words with double consonants.

- Find as many two-syllable words with double consonants as possible, using the letters from the whole-class session.

- Investigate how many members of the class have names with double consonants, e.g. *Rebecca, Hussein, Sally, Tommy, Shirreen*. (This could be extended to relatives, pets, etc.) Prepare a list for classroom display.

- Invent a football team – Consonants Athletic. Draw the team photograph. Give as many players as possible a name that includes a doubled consonant.

- Set a double consonant spelling test for the rest of the class. Try to come up with words that are really tricky! Use a dictionary for help.

REFLECTING: *plenary*

- Share the lists of double consonant words. Focus on interesting and unusual examples.

- Hold the spelling test. Which words are the most difficult?

Resources

Practice PCM 14

ICT

Dictionary

ASSESSMENT
- Spell two-syllable words with double consonants accurately and consistently.
- Find examples of double consonant words and use them accurately in writing.

Spelling revision

2/3

Focus
Word level
Spelling: prefixes
T2/W7

Learning objectives
- to consolidate use of the word *prefix*
- to apply awareness of prefixes to spelling

TEACHING: *whole-class introduction*

Resources

- **Shared text:** use the shared text to identify any words with the prefixes *un-, de-, dis-, re-, pre-*. Recap work from Stage 3 and explain that prefixes make it possible to create new words from root words, e.g. *happy/unhappy, appear/disappear*. Encourage use of the term *prefix*.

  Shared text

- Write up a list of prefixes on the board, including *un-, de-, dis-, re-, pre-, mis-, non-, ex-, co-, anti-, al-*. Ask the children for suggestions for words that use each prefix. These could be written onto the board, and/or written into the class word bank.

- Show how spelling can be made easier by knowing prefixes. Split the children into two groups. Ask one half to spell words from the left-hand column below; the other half from the right. Point out that the root word remains the same each time.

appear	*disappear*
visible	*invisible*
like	*unlike*
happy	*unhappy*
take	*mistake*
ways	*always*
most	*almost*

Spelling revision

DEVELOPING: *group activities*

- Think of as many words as possible that start with one of the following prefixes: *al-, dis-, ex-, sub-, re-, mis- co-*. Use a dictionary for help and prepare to present the words to the rest of the class.◆

- Identify the prefixes in the text. Suggest some new ones and then write some in sentences.◆◆

- Prepare a spelling test for the rest of the class of ten words with prefixes. Use *look, say, cover, write, check* to make sure the group can do its own test.◆◆

- Find out and illustrate on a poster as many prefixes as you can find.◆◆

- Find at least five words where the prefix makes the root word mean the opposite, e.g. *happy/unhappy*. Use each word in a sentence to show that the different meanings of each words are clearly understood.◆◆◆

REFLECTING: *plenary*

- Use the spelling test to check for accurate use of prefixes. Identify and discuss any words that cause particular difficulty.

- Share interesting and unusual examples of words with prefixes that were found during the group activities.

Resources

Dictionary

Textbook page 11

ASSESSMENT
- Recognise and spell words with common prefixes and use the words in context.
- Use the term *prefix*.

Spelling revision

3/3

Focus
Word level
Spelling: contractions
T3/W10

Learning objectives
- to consolidate how apostrophes are used in contracted words
- to distinguish between apostrophes for contraction and possession

TEACHING: *whole-class introduction*

Resources

- Recap the idea from Stage 3 that sometimes words are shortened and an apostrophe is used to show where the letters are missing. Write up (or ask the children to write) some common examples, e.g. *don't, can't, we'll, I've, she's*. Use the terms *apostrophe* and *contraction*.

- **Shared text:** read the Big Book page and ask the children to identify the contracted words (*don't, can't, I'd, isn't, they'll, they've*). Show how some contractions (e.g. *won't* for *will not*) are more difficult to remember.

  Big Book page 5

- Ask for suggestions of other shortened words. Talk about why they are used, e.g. when we talk, we join the sounds of *they are* to make *they're*, and this is reflected in the spelling. (Ask someone to check whether the computer's spell-checker accepts *they're*.)

- Recap the use of the apostrophe for possession. Ask ten volunteers to come out to the front with an object (e.g. pencil, key, shoe, book, etc.) For each, ask someone else to write up the correct use of the apostrophe: e.g. *John's pen; Farouq's key*. Discuss the plural equivalent: *the girls' pens*.

- Explain the difference between *its* (possessive – *the dog slipped its lead*) and *it's* (contraction – *it's hot today*). Note that *its* is an exception to the rule.

Spelling revision

DEVELOPING: *group activities*

Resources

- Make some labels to attach to objects in the classroom showing to whom they belong. Each label must include an apostrophe.◆

- Replace the full forms of words with contracted forms, then write sentences using possessive apostrophes.◆◆

  Textbook page 12

- Write at least five sentences, each using *its* (possession) and *it's* (contraction).◆◆

- As a group, think of as many contractions (*don't, can't*) as possible. Put each one on a separate piece of paper and arrange them as a classroom display.◆◆

- Design a bookmark that includes on it the rules for using apostrophes. Include a note about using *its* and *it's*.◆◆◆

  ICT

REFLECTING: *plenary*

- Begin to make a word bank by putting together the different contracted words from the groups. Consolidate understanding by practising writing the full form of words, starting with the contracted form.

- Recap the rules relating to apostrophes. Ask the children over the next week or so to collect examples of apostrophe mistakes that they see (quote *s'teak and chip's* seen in a restaurant!).

ASSESSMENT
- Investigate the uses of apostrophes and use them appropriately in writing.
- Distinguish between *its* (possession) and *it's* (contraction) and use the two forms correctly.

Dictionaries

1/2

Focus
Word level
Vocabulary: word meanings
T1, 2, 3/revision

Learning objectives
- to develop dictionary skills learned at Stage 3
- to use a dictionary to find or check word meanings

TEACHING: *whole-class introduction*

Resources

- Prompt the children to identify the two main uses of dictionaries: to check meanings and spellings.

- **Shared text:** remind them of earlier work they have done on using dictionaries for the first of these purposes. Use the Big Book page to develop this and recap correct terminology. Draw attention to:
  – the guide word (*club*)
  – the head words (*club*)
  – the part of speech (*noun* and *verb*)
  – the definition(s): prompt them to look at the style in which these are written (eg. not complete sentences, definitions of verbs usually begin with the word *to*); use the term *definition*
  – the numbered listing of definitions of words with more than one meaning
  – the listing at the end of the entry of words that are derived from the head word (this point is a focus of the second session).

  Big Book page 6

- Look at the dictionary normally used in the class, and compare an entry with those in the Big Book. This should include the features listed above, but there may well be minor differences of treatment and layout for the children to identify.

  Dictionary

- Work through the process of finding a word in the class dictionary. Consider issues of clarity and precision in definitions.

Dictionaries

DEVELOPING: *group activities*

Note: one or more dictionaries will need to be available to each group during this part of the session.

- Write definitions of common words. Compare them with those in the class dictionary and identify similarities and differences.◆

- As above, but use a text from a novel or information book they are currently reading. Choose words that are tricky or challenging and prepare to present them to the rest of the class.◆◆

- Write definitions for words with more than one meaning. Compare their definitions with those in the dictionary.◆◆

- Read a text including unusual and challenging vocabulary. Use the context to try to work out the meaning. Write definitions and check them in the dictionary.◆◆◆

REFLECTING: *plenary*

- Share definitions they have written: which are the clearest and most helpful? What is difficult about writing definitions?

- Share unusual words they have found, and discuss their meanings. Discuss strategies for remembering the meanings, e.g. including them in the class word bank.

Resources

Practice PCM 15

ICT
Reading book

Practice PCM 16

Textbook page 13

ASSESSMENT
- Understand and use the term *definition*.
- Use dictionaries effectively to find and check word meanings.

Dictionaries

2/2

Focus
Word level
Vocabulary: word spellings
T1, 2, 3/revision

Learning objectives
- to use dictionaries to check spellings
- to develop strategies for finding difficult or unusual words

TEACHING: *whole-class introduction*

Resources

- **Shared text:** look again at the Big Book page and ask the children how they would go about using a dictionary to check the spelling of a word. Reinforce earlier work on alphabetical organisation by initial and subsequent letters. How do guide words help in this process? (They can help guide you to approximately the right place in the dictionary.)

  Big Book page 6

- Explain that, although this is usually straightforward, there are two common complications.
  1) Words do not begin with the expected letter, such as *knee*. You will not find this word when looking under *n*, which from the sound of the word seems to be its first letter. Illustrate this with the sound of hard *c*, as in *cat*. This is usually represented by the letter *c*. How else can it be spelt? Guide children to *k* (as in *kite*) and *ch* (as in *choir*). Stress how useful knowing this is when checking spellings: if you have looked up a word under a letter but cannot find it or are not sure how a word begins, think of the possibilities.
  2) The word you are looking up is not a head word. Write up the word *pollution* as an example. Explain that the word *pollution* is not a head word; to find it, you have to know or work out the root word on which it is based (*pollute*). Relate this to work on word endings. Work through the process of finding other derived words (e.g. *jewellery*).

Dictionaries

DEVELOPING: *group activities*

Resources

Note: one or more dictionaries will need to be available to each group during this part of the session.

- Use a dictionary to find words beginning with these sounds: *ph-* (sounds like *f*, e.g. *photograph*) and *wh-* (sounds like *w*, e.g. *when*). Write lists of words for classroom display, as a reminder of tricky spellings.◆

ICT

- Examine picture clues for words that begin with unexpected letters. Write each word, check the spelling in a dictionary, and explain what is unusual about each example.◆◆

Textbook page 14

- Identify the headword under which you would have to look to find given derived words.◆◆◆

Practice PCM 17

- List possible words under a given headword. Check in the class dictionary, identifying those which have their own entry and those which do not.◆◆◆

Practice PCM 18

REFLECTING: *plenary*

- Share lists of words that begin with *ch-*, *ph-* or *th-*. Which words are the most difficult to spell?

- Explain how the class dictionary handles words in the same family. What is helpful/unhelpful about this?

Homework

- Work out the meanings of new words in a text, and then check against dictionary definitions.◆◆

Homework PCM 8

ASSESSMENT
- Use dictionaries effectively and accurately to check spellings.
- Develop strategies for checking spellings of unusual and tricky words.

Word puzzles

1/3

Focus
Word level
Vocabulary: pattern and rhyme
T1, 2, 3/revision, T1/W13

Learning objectives
- to use word play to extend knowledge of spelling patterns and rhyme
- to identify and explore unconventional spellings

TEACHING: *whole-class introduction*

Resources

- **Shared text:** use some simple rhyming poems to remind the children how rhyme and word play can be used for humour. Identify words that are spelt differently but still rhyme (e.g. *come/mum*).

  Big Book page 26

- Explain and work through examples of the following word play activities. Identify and discuss how they relate to learning about spelling and vocabulary.
  1) *Number plates.* Make words using the letters of vehicle registration numbers. Write down some examples (real and/or invented). Can the letters be arranged to make a word? What words can be made if other letters are added? Who can make the most words in a minute? Who can make the longest word?
  2) *Guess the rhyme.* Someone thinks of a word with several rhymes (e.g. *sock*), and says: "I'm thinking of a word that rhymes with *knock*." Others try to guess the word by asking questions like "Does it tell the time?" The puzzle-setter answers by saying "no, it's not a *clock*." Compile a list of rhyming words. Refer to a rhyming dictionary.

     Rhyming dictionary

  3) *Unconventional spellings.* Explain that sometimes people spell words wrongly on purpose! Give some examples (see Textbook page 15 for ideas). Ask: *How should these words be spelt? Where do you see spellings like this? What is the reason for doing it?* Can they think of any other examples?

     Textbook page 15

Word puzzles

DEVELOPING: *group activities*

- Compile lists of rhyming words and use them to play *Guess the rhyme* as a group.◆

- List words that can be made from the letters on car number plates.◆◆

- Find other examples of unconventional spellings in names of products and businesses. Catalogues and telephone directories are good sources. For each example, write the correct spelling of the word.◆◆

- Investigate unconventional spellings. Identify the correct spelling pattern.◆◆

- Find or invent other words with unconventional spellings, e.g. for a new product or service. The children could try to combine unconventional spellings with rhyme, e.g. *Soopa Snoopas – Detective Agency*. Prepare a list for display, showing the correct spelling alongside each example.◆◆◆

Resources

Rhyming dictionary

Practice PCM 19

Catalogues Directories

Textbook page 15

ICT

REFLECTING: *plenary*

- Share interesting examples of words from number plates or lists of rhyming words.

- Share found or invented words with unconventional spellings.

Homework

Find names of animals in a wordsearch, some with unusual spellings (e.g. *llama*).◆◆

Homework PCM 9

ASSESSMENT
- Identify unconventional spellings and provide correct versions.
- Use rhyme and word play to help remember spelling patterns.

Word puzzles

2/3

Focus
Word level
Vocabulary: alphabetical order
T1/W12

Learning objectives
- to organise words alphabetically, using third and subsequent letters
- to locate words in alphabetically-ordered texts

TEACHING: *whole-class introduction*

Resources: a collection of books and catalogues with substantial indexes; other alphabetically-organised material, e.g. telephone books, guide books, encyclopaedias.

Resources

- **Shared text:** use a dictionary or an encyclopaedia to remind the children about alphabetically-ordered texts. Ask them how texts like this are organised (by initial letter, then second, then third, etc).

Shared text

- Write up six words or names in which either the first two or the first three letters are the same; make sure they are not in alphabetical order. Indexes from books or catalogues provide a good source for this, e.g. *seals, seasons, seaweed, seeds, Senegal, senses.*

- Prompt the children to explain how to sort them into alphabetical order, and work together to produce an alphabetical listing.

- Ask each child to write on a small piece of paper a word beginning with the same two given letters, making sure that it is a combination which begins a large number of words, e.g. a consonant blend or consonant plus vowel. Ask them to check their spelling with a partner, and correct it if necessary. Then ask them to hold up their words and sort themselves into alphabetical order.

Word puzzles

DEVELOPING: *group activities*

- Place words in the correct gaps in an index, sorting by third and fourth letters.◆

- Sort names of children's authors into alphabetical order.◆◆

- Compile a list of words beginning with the same three letters, e.g. *tra, def, cha, com, sat*. Then sort the words into alphabetical order, and/or write them on pieces of card for the rest of the children to use in the sorting game from the whole-class session.◆◆

- Design and produce a simple poster for the classroom, explaining how to locate and organise words in alphabetical order. Include a range of examples.◆◆

- Investigate indexes and other alphabetically-organised material in the class collection; be ready to demonstrate, explain and evaluate how they work.◆◆◆

Resources

Practice PCM 20

Practice PCM 21

Dictionary

ICT

Reference books

REFLECTING: *plenary*

- Play the alphabetical ordering game again, using the sets of words the children have compiled.

- Present an explanation and demonstration of the alphabetically-organised material that has been investigated.

ASSESSMENT
- Locate words in alphabetically-ordered texts by third and fourth letters.
- Sort words alphabetically by third and fourth letters.

Word puzzles

3/3

Focus
Text level
Vocabulary: explaining words
T1/W11, T2/W12

Learning objectives
- to define familiar vocabulary in their own words
- to investigate the formation and use of invented words

TEACHING: *whole-class introduction*

Resources

- **Shared text:** use the shared text to identify a number of familiar words, e.g. *car, telephone, house, school, sister, brother*. Write up a list of the words and ask volunteers to define each one in their own words.

  Shared text

- The children might find this very difficult and find that their definitions go on for a long time! Try playing the Definition Game: in pairs or groups, the children have to define familiar words in a set number of words, e.g. *'Define 'car' in five words'* – *'adults drive these on roads'*. Point out that the fewer the words, the harder it gets!

- Discuss how this could help the children's writing for different purposes, e.g. in a story they might use a long description, but in a business letter they would need to keep descriptions short. This helps to keep the reader's interest.

- Some authors even use completely invented words to get their ideas across as quickly and powerfully as possible. Read the first verse of Lewis Carroll's *The Jabberwocky* from the Anthology. Encourage the children to share their ideas about what is going on. What scene do they see? What atmosphere is conveyed? What makes it impossible to know for sure?

  Anthology page 37

- Write up some of the invented words and discuss what they might mean.

48

Word puzzles

DEVELOPING: *group activities*

- Write dictionary entries for at least three of the invented words in the poem. If you have a copy of Lewis Carroll's *Through the Looking Glass*, read the children the text in Chapter 6 where Humpty explains the meaning of these words.◆

- Re-read the first verse of *The Jabberwocky* and attempt to define some of the words. Invent words to describe a friend.◆◆

- Invent new words to describe an invented creature.◆◆

- Play the Definition Game (vary this according to the ability level of the children).◆◆/◆◆◆
  - define using four words: *television, dog, football*
  - define using three words: *house, carpet, window*
  - define using two words: *pen, ruler, desk, school*
  - define using one word: *computer, mouse, screen*

REFLECTING: *plenary*

- Share definitions for the invented words: Which are plausible/implausible? Why? Which is the best? Why?

- Discuss the results of the Definitions Game. Discuss how practice with short descriptions like this might help the children in their own writing.

Homework
- Write clues to help remember tricky spellings.◆◆

Resources

Anthology page 37

Practice PCM 22

Textbook page 16

Homework PCM 10

ASSESSMENT
- Define familiar vocabulary in a limited number of words.
- Investigate meanings and definitions using invented words.

New words

Focus
Word level
Vocabulary: alternative words
T2/W9

Learning objectives
- to improve children's choice of vocabulary
- to use words that are more accurate and interesting than common choices

TEACHING: *whole-class introduction*

Resources

- Ask the children to write down on a piece of paper how many words they think they know (a good estimate is 300 at age 2; 5,000 at age 5, and 12,000 at age 12). Compare the results. Discuss how they learn new words, e.g. from talking, reading, looking at words around them every day, etc.

- One way of learning new words is by building from other words. Revise work from previous sessions, e.g.:
  - compound words: *blackbird, haircut, football, headache, classroom*
  - word families: *help, helpless, helpful, helper, unhelpful, helping.*

- **Shared text:** use the shared text to introduce the idea of using new or interesting words instead of the usual choices. For example, authors use many words instead of *said: called, whispered, shouted, exclaimed, gasped.* Explain that each of the alternative words is carefully chosen, depending on the meaning the author wants to get across. What other examples can the children suggest?

  Shared text

- Discuss how alternative words could be used in their own writing. Write up the sentence *She is a nice girl.* Ask the children for suggestions for alternatives to the word *nice*, e.g. *pretty, good, helpful, kind.*

New words

DEVELOPING: *group activities*

- How many alternative words can the group suggest for *funny, sad, clever, and large*? Use a dictionary.◆

- Play the ten-minute word race: use a dictionary or thesaurus to find as many words as possible as alternatives for *good*. Then spend the next ten minutes using each alternative word in a sentence, to show that each meaning is understood.◆◆

- Introduce the idea of 'Today's New Word' – to be posted by a different child at the start of each school day. Discuss how it will be chosen and why, how it will be displayed and illustrated, and what sorts of word will be chosen. This could be linked to current topic work.◆◆

- Rewrite a postcard, using more interesting and accurate words to replace the underlined words.◆◆

- Use a current reading book or topic book to find good examples of alternative and interesting words being used. Prepare some examples for classroom display.◆◆◆

REFLECTING: *plenary*

- Discuss the plans for 'Today's New Word' and share examples found from current reading and topic books.

- Share the words found in the ten-minute word race.

Resources

Dictionary

Dictionary
Thesaurus

Practice
PCM 23

ICT

Reading
book

ASSESSMENT
- Use alternative words and expressions to add interest to writing.
- Develop strategies for building up a personal and class vocabulary.

New words

Focus
Word level
Vocabulary: changing words
T2/W11

Learning objectives
- to explore how vocabulary changes over time
- to collect words that have become little used and discuss why

TEACHING: *whole-class introduction*

Resources

- **Shared text:** use the shared text to focus on common words that have multiple meanings, e.g. *coat* (a layer of paint, a jacket, an animal's fur, etc). Lead into a discussion about how some common words have been used for a long time, while the use of some words changes over time.

  Shared text

- Ask the children if they know the meaning of the following words: *wireless, frock, pantry, shilling, spectacles*. Explain that these words have become little used, for various reasons:
  - technical words now replaced: *radio* for *wireless*
  - words changed with fashions: *dress* for *frock*
  - words with simpler versions: *glasses* for *spectacles*
  - words that change because of the way we live: houses no longer have a *pantry*, *shillings* are no longer a type of money.

- Can the children think of any other examples of words that have become little used? They may have come across examples in their reading, or heard older relatives using unusual words.

- Ask the children to suggest words or expressions that are quite new to the language. These are often to do with technology, e.g. *telephone, television, Internet, CD-ROM, laptop, download, laser,* or words borrowed from other languages, e.g. *poppadam, Diwali*.

New words

DEVELOPING: *group activities*

Resources

- Follow on from the whole-class activity: collect all the words discussed that have changed over time (e.g. *wireless*) and make a list for display. Some of the words could be illustrated to help explain them.◆

ICT

- Begin a class database of words that have changed in use over time. Decide which words will be included – words that are never used today, or words that are still sometimes used? Use a dictionary.◆◆

ICT

Dictionary

- Write the beginning of a story, using as many old words from the whole-class session as possible. Make sure the meanings are understood!◆◆

- Find as many new words as possible. Use five to ten of the new words (e.g. *laptop, laser*) in sentences to show that their meaning is understood.◆◆

Dictionary

- Choose five to ten of the old words discussed at the beginning of the session, and suggest reasons why each word is no longer used, e.g. *shillings aren't used any more.*◆◆◆

REFLECTING: *plenary*

- Share ideas for collecting changed words in a word bank or database.

- Discuss examples of old and new words being used in sentences. Does everyone agree that the meaning of each word is clear? If not, how could the sentences be improved?

ASSESSMENT
- Recognise that language changes over time and discuss why.
- Explore use of old and new words and understand their meanings.

Transforming words

Focus
Word level
Vocabulary: gender
T2/W10

Learning objectives
- to recognise that some words imply gender
- to investigate the formation of such words, e.g. *prince/princess*

TEACHING: *whole-class introduction*

Resources

- **Shared text:** use the shared text to identify nouns that imply gender. Start with simple nouns, e.g. *boy/girl*. Explain that this is an example where the male and female versions are completely different words, but in some cases the female version of a word is formed by adding *-ess*, e.g. *prince/princess*.

    Shared text

- Write up a list of words that have alternative gender forms, e.g. *prince, girl, woman, cow, fox, king, brother, daughter*. Ask the children to supply the alternative forms (in this case, *princess, boy, man, bull, vixen, queen, sister, son*).

- Introduce the suffix *-ess*; give some examples where it denotes gender: *actress, stewardess,* and *princess*.

- Write up ten words and cover them. Reveal each one and ask the children to decide if the word describes a male, female, or both: *lion, cat, doctor, nurse, pilot, engineer, fox, duke, scientist, chairman*. Then ask them which ones can change to become male or female. (In this case, *lion/lioness, fox/vixen, duke/duchess, chairman/chairwoman*.)

- Introduce the idea that some words are used today that deliberately do not tell you whether they are male or female (often words to do with jobs, e.g. *police officer, fire fighter, chairperson*). This is so that the words include both males and females.

Transforming words

DEVELOPING: *group activities*

- Find male or female partners for the list of examples. ◆

- Find five to ten words which can be changed by adding *-ess*. Write each word in a sentence to show that the meaning is understood. ◆

- Write a list of animals that might be found on a farm, e.g. *pigs, cows, horses, dogs, sheep.* Find out which animal names have male and female forms, and write them, e.g. *pig/sow.* ◆◆

- Produce a list of words that are often thought of as male, but could equally be female (e.g. *engineer*), or the other way around (e.g. *nurse*). Use a dictionary for help. ◆◆◆

- Write a list of jobs that do not imply gender, e.g. *fire fighter, police officer, head teacher.* Make the list as long as possible! ◆◆◆

REFLECTING: *plenary*

- Share the list of animals and their male/female forms. Can the rest of the class think of any other examples?

- As a class, write a list of words ending in *-ess*, drawing on the words produced in the group activities.

Resources

Practice PCM 24

Reference books

Dictionary

ASSESSMENT
- Understand the gender implications of certain words and how they are formed.
- Use and spell such words accurately.

Transforming words

2/3

Focus
Word level
Vocabulary: making verbs and adjectives
T1/W14, T2/W13

Learning objectives
- to recognise how nouns and adjectives can make verbs
- to recognise how nouns and verbs can make adjectives

TEACHING: *whole-class introduction*

Resources

- **Shared text:** remind the children of the difference between verbs ('doing' or 'being' words), nouns ('naming' words), and adjectives ('describing' words). Read a short text together, and identify examples of each.

    Shared text

- Explain that some nouns and adjectives can be turned into verbs by adding suffixes. e.g.:
  – nouns: *drama – dramatise; decor – decorate*
  – verbs: *simple – simplify; weak – weaken*.
  Briefly discuss the spelling rules for adding word endings (see page 28). What other examples can the children suggest?

- Write up a list of simple adjectives with suffixes, e.g. *-ful: careful, helpful, boastful, cheerful, colourful*. Point out that in each case a suffix has been added to a noun or a verb to make an adjective. Discuss which suffixes are added more frequently than others (e.g. *-ful* is added quite frequently, but others less so: *-ic, -able, -ing, -like*).

- Introduce the children to the Adjective Generator: a box with three sections: verbs, nouns and suffixes. Write examples of each word type on cards (using ideas above) and put them in the Generator. Individuals then withdraw a verb or noun plus suffix. See how many adjectives are generated in this way. (This could of course be varied to make a Verb Generator.)

Transforming words

DEVELOPING: *group activities*

- Use the Adjective Generator (or Verb Generator) to make some adjectives (or verbs). Write a list of the completed adjectives (or verbs).◆

- Create adjectives by adding endings to lists of words.◆◆

- Choose three of the suffixes discussed with the whole class and make up as many verbs or adjectives as possible using them.◆◆

- Select ten of the verbs and adjectives discussed in the whole-class session. Use each example in a sentence to show that the meaning is fully understood.◆◆

- Poster challenge: invent ten new verbs or adjectives using suffixes. Include them in a list on a poster with ten 'real' examples. The challenge for the rest of the class is to work out which verbs or adjectives are 'real' and which are invented.◆◆◆

REFLECTING: *plenary*

- Discuss the finished poster and decide together which examples are 'real' and which are invented.

- Share the words produced by the Adjective Generator (or Verb Generator).

Homework

- Transform nouns and verbs into adjectives.◆◆

Resources

Practice
PCM 25

ICT

Homework
PCM 11

ASSESSMENT

- Recognise that suffixes can be used to change nouns and adjectives into verbs, and nouns and verbs to adjectives.
- Use this understanding to develop and extend personal vocabulary.

Transforming words

3/3

Focus
Word level
Vocabulary: diminutive words
T3/W12

Learning objectives
- to investigate different ways to make words signifying smaller size
- to recognise and use a range of diminutives

TEACHING: *whole-class introduction*

Resources

- **Shared text:** use the shared text to locate any examples of diminutives. Explain that these are words that suggest smallness:
  - using an adjective: *little boy*
  - by adding a prefix or suffix: *minicab, starlet*
  - nouns: *sapling*
  - nicknames: *Jonesy.*

Shared text

- Which members of the class have nicknames? Discuss each one in turn. Which is the shortest, the furthest from their real name, etc? Write up a list of diminutive nicknames, e.g. Pete, Stevie, Baz.

- Discuss adjectives that can be used to describe smallness, e.g. *tiny, little, small*. Discuss examples that the children might have come across in their reading, e.g. *Tiny Tim*.

- Write up these words on the board: *car, bus, van, computer, kitchen, wave, drop, cab*. Ask for suggestions for making each of these suggest smaller size using a prefix or suffix:
  - ***mini-*** *cab, bus, van, car*
  - ***micro-*** *computer, wave*
  - ***-ette*** *kitchenette*
  - ***-let*** *droplet.*

  Discuss other suffixes, e.g. *-kin*. Point out, though, that *catkin* isn't a small cat!

Transforming words

DEVELOPING: *group activities*

Resources

- Find at least five examples of words that suggest reduced size. Write each word in a sentence to show that the meaning is understood.

  Dictionary

- Plan a survey of nicknames. Work with a partner to find out information around the school about nicknames. Use the computer to store and present the data. Distinguish between shortened real names and made-up nicknames.

- Make up a list of football, rugby league or American football teams. Change the names to suggest smallness. For example, the *Pittsburgh Steelettes* (*Steelers*), the *Bradford Bullkins* (*Bulls*).

- Write five to ten sentences about how the world would look if you were a giant, e.g. including *little buildings*, *tiny trees*. Use a dictionary or thesaurus for help.

  Dictionary
  Thesaurus

- Write the beginning of a story where the central character finds him or herself in a magical world where everything has suddenly become much smaller. Include at least five examples of diminutives discussed in the whole-class session.

REFLECTING: *plenary*

- Discuss the story openings. Tell the children briefly about the story of *Gulliver's Travels*.

- Share the plans for and results of the nickname survey.

ASSESSMENT

- Recognise and use different ways of forming diminutives.
- Use diminutives accurately in writing.

Parts of speech

1/2

Focus

Sentence level
Grammar: nouns,
pronouns, verbs, adjectives
T1, 2, 3/revision

Learning objectives

- to consolidate knowledge of nouns, pronouns, verbs, and adjectives
- to use such terminology confidently

TEACHING: *whole-class introduction*

Resources

- **Shared text:** use the shared text to briefly recap on examples of nouns, pronouns, verbs and adjectives. Find examples of each and discuss them. Ask the children if there are any areas they are unsure about, and clarify them.

  Shared text

- Split the class into four groups, each responsible for nouns, pronouns, verbs or adjectives. Set the challenge: each group has five minutes to find and list as many nouns, pronouns, verbs and adjectives as possible from the evidence in the classroom, books in the class library, and so on.

- Collect examples from each group. Write them for display, either on the board or on large sheets of paper that can be pinned up. Discuss each set of examples and point out that some words could be in more than one group, e.g. some nouns are also verbs.

- Ask each group to come up with a short written definition for 'their' part of speech. Check that each definition is correct (e.g. *a noun is the name of a person, place or thing; a verb is a 'doing' or 'being' word*).

Parts of speech

DEVELOPING: *group activities*

Resources

- Finish each sentences by adding one word, then identify which part of speech it is.

Practice PCM 26

- Practise identifying nouns, verbs and adjectives in the poem, then write a new verse.

Textbook page 17

- Look back at a recent piece of written work and identify where nouns, pronouns, verbs and adjectives have been used. Improve the writing if necessary, e.g. check for accurate use of pronouns.

Recent work

- From the headlines in a recent newspaper, cut out at least five examples and annotate them to show nouns, verbs, adjectives and pronouns. Stick them on a poster for display.

Newspapers

- Write a script for a three-minute television or radio advertisement selling and explaining parts of speech. Rehearse it and prepare for a presentation to the rest of the class.

ICT

REFLECTING: *plenary*

- Present the advertisements that sell or explain parts of speech.

- Look at the newspaper headline extracts and use them to clear up any remaining confusion about nouns, pronouns, verbs and adjectives.

Homework

- Insert the correct pronouns into the sentences.

Homework PCM 12

ASSESSMENT

- Recognise and use basic parts of speech accurately.
- Use the correct terminology: *noun*, *pronoun*, *verb* and *adjective*.

Parts of speech

2/2

Focus
Sentence level
Grammar: nouns,
pronouns, verbs, adjectives
T1, 2, 3/revision

Learning objectives
- to consolidate knowledge of basic parts of speech
- to recognise more complex uses of nouns and adjectives

TEACHING: *whole-class introduction*

Resources

- Remind the children about the basic parts of speech they revised in the previous session: nouns, pronouns, verbs and adjectives.

- Split the class into groups of three. Each group should invent a sentence containing a noun, verb and adjective. Listen to, and comment on, each sentence.

- **Shared text:** read the extract from *How the Whale Became and Other Stories* in the Big Book. Focus on nouns: *birds, feathers, feet*. The children should recognise these as 'straightforward' nouns as they have defined them: *the name of a person, place or thing*. Then look at the word *darkness*. Explain that this is a noun, even though it is not a person, place or really a 'thing'. You cannot hold it, pick it up or do anything with it: it is an *abstract noun*. Discuss other examples, e.g. *happiness, sadness, other feelings, ideas*, etc.

  Big Book page 7

- Look at the expression *the new country* at the end of the first paragraph. The children should recognise *new* as a 'straightforward' adjective, placed before the noun. Then look at the first sentence: *The birds grew thin*. Ask the children which word is the adjective (*thin*) and stress that adjectives do not always have to be in front of the noun. Ask them to think of other examples, e.g. *The girl was tall; The dog was smelly; The car was so clean it shone.*

Parts of speech

DEVELOPING: *group activities*

- Write five to ten simple sentences using adjectives that are not in front of the noun, e.g. *The cat was black. The class is noisy.*◆

- Follow on from the whole-class session by listing as many abstract nouns as possible. Collect them on to a poster for display.◆◆

- Using a favourite reading book or other text, find examples of nouns and/or adjectives used in the way discussed with the whole class. Be ready to share examples.◆◆

- Identify nouns, pronouns, verbs and adjectives in a text extract, including abstract nouns and adjectives that are remote from the nouns they are describing. ◆◆

- Write the opening of a story called *Nigel and the Noun Factory*, where Nigel has to sort out abstract nouns, proper nouns and common nouns. Include examples of each kind of noun. Use a dictionary for help.◆◆◆

Resources

Dictionary

ICT

Reading books

Textbook page 18

Dictionary

REFLECTING: *plenary*

- Share the simple sentences containing adjectives and write more to add to the list.

- Share and discuss examples of nouns and adjectives found in reading books. Which examples does the class like best?

ASSESSMENT
- Use knowledge of basic parts of speech confidently and accurately.
- Recognise and use more complex forms of nouns and adjectives.

Verbs

Focus
Sentence level
Grammar: verbs (revision)
T1, 2, 3/revision, T1/S2

Learning objectives
- to recognise the purpose and function of verbs
- to use the term *verb* appropriately

TEACHING: *whole-class introduction*

Resources

- **Shared text:** identify basic verbs in sentences. Remind the children of the basic definition of a verb (*a 'doing' or 'being' word*) and write up lists of examples.

Shared text

- Write up the following sentences (or similar):
  – *Go to the door and open it.*
  – *The sun shines and the grass is green.*
  – *The boys played games and the girls kicked a ball.*
  Read each sentence in turn and ask the children to identify each verb. Rub out or cover up each verb as it is identified: *go, open, shines, is, played, kicked*. Ask the children to read together the remaining words from each sentence, to emphasise that sentences do not make sense without verbs.

- Ask the children to suggest replacement verbs for each sentence and discuss how each new verb changes the sentence meaning, e.g. *Walk to the door and pull it.* Explain that some words can be nouns as well as verbs, e.g. *He runs; He goes for a run.*

- Examine the difference between the third sentence above and the other two. Remind the children of their work on tenses from Stage 3 and draw out the fact that the action described by the verbs in this sentence has already happened – so the verbs have *-ed* on the end. Remind them of the term *tense*. Stress that not all verbs end like this in the past tense (e.g. *run/ran*).

Verbs

DEVELOPING: *group activities*

- Using a favourite reading book, look for interesting or unusual examples of verbs. Write a list and prepare to present the results to the rest of the class.◆

- Write three simple sentences (like the examples in the whole-class session), then write them again, using different verbs. Discuss how the new verbs have changed the meaning of the sentences.◆◆

- Prepare a poster for display that explains all about verbs and how they can be used. Include plenty of examples and use illustrations.◆◆

- With a partner, find an extract from a story you both like. Write out four or five lines of it, but remove the verbs and leave spaces instead. Then, ask two other children to guess what the verbs are. Check their answers.◆◆

- Look at a list of words that can be both verbs and nouns. Write sentences that show the difference between them.◆◆◆

REFLECTING: *plenary*

- Share and discuss the interesting and unusual examples of verbs from reading books.

- Discuss words that can be both verbs and nouns. Write a list of as many examples as possible.

Resources

Reading book

Reading book

ICT

Textbook page 19

ASSESSMENT
- Use the term *verb* accurately.
- Understand the function of verbs in sentences and use them accurately.

Verbs

2/4

Focus

Sentence level
Grammar: tenses – basic
T1/S2

Learning objectives

- to understand and use the term *tense* in relation to verbs
- to distinguish between past, present and future tenses

TEACHING: *whole-class introduction*

Resources

- Recap the definition of a *verb* (*a 'doing' or 'being' word*) and *tense* (*this tells us when something is happening – past, present or future*).

- **Shared text:** share the Big Book page with the children. Ask them to identify the verbs. Recap on Stage 3 work and talk about how stories are usually in the past tense, and how past tenses often use *-ed* (e.g. *squirmed, wriggled*). Find and discuss the irregular past-tense forms (e.g. *didn't, kept, found, took, fell, began, saw*).

- Together, read through the text again, but this time change every verb to the present tense as each sentence is read. Discuss how this affects the story. Show how one way of deciding whether a word is a verb or not is testing whether or not its tense can be changed.

> Big Book page 8

- Introduce the idea of the future tense and stress that this is used for things that will (or might) happen in the future. Give an example by reading the first few sentences of the Big Book text in the future tense: *He will squirm and he will wriggle …* Discuss different forms, e.g. *I will, I shall, I am going to*.

- Shared writing: together, write a present-tense sentence, and then write its past and future forms.

Verbs

DEVELOPING: *group activities*

Resources

- Use a favourite reading book to find examples of past, present and future tenses. Prepare to present some example sentences to the rest of the class.◆

  Reading books

- Read a short text about a squirrel story and identify the verb tenses (past, present and future).◆◆

  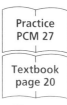

- Choose the correct verb tense for each sentence, then correct tense errors in a short text.◆◆

- Find ten irregular past-tense verbs (use the Big Book text for ideas). Write them in a list and add the present and future forms of each example.◆◆

- Design and produce a simple poster for display that could be used as a quick reminder to the class about past, present and future tenses.◆◆◆

REFLECTING: *plenary*

- Present examples of different tenses from reading books. Do the class agree that these are good examples of each tense?

- Present the poster as a reminder of their work on tenses. Do the children find it helpful? How could it be improved?

Homework

- Rewrite sentences about Amy's holiday in the past tense.◆

  Homework PCM 13

ASSESSMENT
- Understand and use the term *tense*.
- Investigate and distinguish between past, present and future tenses.

Verbs

3/4

Focus
Sentence level
Grammar: using tenses
T1/S2

Learning objectives
- to investigate how the tense of a verb can depend on the purpose of the writing
- to use such understanding in writing

Resources

TEACHING: *whole-class introduction*

- **Shared text:** compare the six sentences in the Big Book. Ask the children to identify verbs and their tenses, and then talk about where they think those sentences come from (story, weather forecast, notice, textbook, instructions, directions).

Big Book page 9

- Discuss how the tense can give a clue to the purpose of the text, e.g.:
  - stories are usually in the past tense
  - explanations, instructions and notices are usually in the present tense
  - forecasts and directions are usually in the future tense.

- Reinforce this point by experimenting with some of the tenses on the Big Book page. For example, the weather forecast wouldn't make sense in the past: *The weather was stormy over the next 24 hours*; the story would be silly in the future tense: *The car will come to a halt suddenly*. Ask the children for their own ideas for silly tense changes!

Big Book page 9

- Shared writing: together, write (a) a letter complaining about something; or (b) instructions for the route of a cycle race or car rally; or (c) a weather forecast. Discuss which tenses work best in each set of circumstances.

Verbs

DEVELOPING: *group activities*

Resources

- Correct the tense errors in a range of sentences, then identify the correct tense for each: past, present or future.◆

  Practice PCM 28

- Correct the tense errors in a letter from a Spanish penfriend, then write back to explain how to use verb tenses.◆◆

  Textbook page 21

- Write one of the following: a weather forecast, a set of instructions, or a match report. Identify which verb tense needs to be used, and keep it consistent. Underline the verbs in the finished work.◆◆

- Design and produce a simple poster for the classroom that explains all three tenses and describes the kinds of texts they are usually used for.◆◆

- Choose one of the text types discussed with the whole class (e.g. notices, instructions, directions, but not stories) and find as many examples as possible in and around the school. Identify the verb tenses and prepare to share the examples.◆◆◆

REFLECTING: *plenary*

- Present the posters with examples of tenses and text types. Can anything be added or improved?

- Share and discuss examples of text types found in and around the school. Are there any exceptions to the examples discussed at the beginning of the session?

ASSESSMENT
- Relate verb tenses to the purpose and structure of different texts.
- Use this understanding effectively in writing.

Verbs

4/4

Focus

Sentence level
Grammar: powerful verbs
T1/S3

Learning objectives

- to recognise the range and potential of verbs
- to use powerful verbs in writing

TEACHING: *whole-class introduction*

Resources

- Recap the definition of a verb as a 'doing' or 'being' word. Take someone's first name (e.g. *Shireen*) and ask the children to suggest verbs beginning with each letter, e.g. *s, h, i,* and so on.

- Ask a volunteer to walk over to the door. Write up *X walked to the door.* Ask him or her to go the door again, but walking differently this time. Change the verb to match the walk, e.g. *X limped to the door.* See how many variations the children can find. Talk about the importance of using different verbs, and give examples: *chuckled* for *laughed, hobbled* for *went,* and so on.

- **Shared text:** using the Big Book page, cover the list of verbs and ask the children to suggest 'new' verbs to replace those underlined in the text. Later, reveal the words Gene Kemp actually wrote.

  Big Book
  page 10

- Write four verbs (*said, went, put, got*) separately on cards and put them in a box or hat. Ask someone to pull out one verb: they have to think of a more powerful version of the verb (e.g. *called* for *said*). Then the rest of the class should suggest a sentence using that verb.

- Shared writing: write up the sentences and discuss further alternatives to the verbs suggested.

Verbs

DEVELOPING: *group activities*

- Follow on from the whole-class session by writing sentences using alternatives for *said, went, put, got*. How many sentences can be written in 20 minutes?◆

- Find new and powerful verbs to replace underlined words in the text, using a thesaurus for help.◆◆

- Find 5-10 newspaper headlines. Cut out the verbs and put in new ones. Prepare the new headlines for a class display.◆◆

- With a partner, find a piece of fiction writing where you think the writer has used powerful and exciting verbs. Prepare a reading of part of this.◆◆

- Choose either *went, put, got, said* or *laughed*. See how many alternatives you can think of (in five minutes!). Use a dictionary or thesaurus for help. Then choose five examples and write them in sentences to show the meaning is understood.◆◆◆

REFLECTING: *plenary*

- Share and discuss the sentences using alternatives for *said, went, put, got*. Hold a vote to decide the most interesting, powerful and effective verb that has been used.

- Discuss the newspaper headlines. Do the new verbs fit? Could they be improved?

Resources

Textbook page 22

Thesaurus

ICT

Story books

Dictionary
Thesaurus

ASSESSMENT
- Recognise how powerful verbs can be used in writing.
- Use powerful verbs appropriately and effectively in writing.

Adverbs

1/2

Focus
Sentence level
Grammar: basic adverbs
T1/S4

Learning objectives
- to identify and understand the function of adverbs
- to learn and use related spelling patterns

TEACHING: *whole-class introduction*

Resources

- **Shared text:** Read through the first sentence, and draw children's attention to the first adverb (*quickly*). Ask them what information this word gives us. Explain that it describes how a particular action is performed and gives more information about a verb.

- Ask the children what they notice about the parts of this word. Guide them to the idea that it is composed of two parts: an adjective (*quick*) plus the suffix *-ly*.

Big Book page 11

- Read through the rest of the Big Book text, prompting children to identify the adverbs, and to explain what information they provide. Discuss their impact on the meaning of the sentence by re-reading part of the text without the adverbs: what effect does this have? (Text is less interesting, less clear, etc.)

- Explain that adverbs are usually formed by adding *-ly* to an adjective. Draw out the spelling rules:
  - *-le* ending: drop the *e* before adding *-ly*
  - *-y* ending: change *y* to *i* before adding *-ly*.
  Illustrate with further examples, e.g. *simple, terrible, sensible, cheeky, lazy, angry, noisy*.

- Brainstorm lists of adverbs that can be used to describe particular actions (e.g. *walking, eating, talking*) or, more challengingly, concepts (e.g. *speed, light, sound*).

Adverbs

DEVELOPING: *group activities*

- Read an extract from a story or information book currently in use. Identify and list the adverbs and prepare to present the list to the rest of the class.◆

- Add *-ly* to turn a list of adjectives into adverbs, following spelling rules for adjectives ending in *-le* and *-y*.◆

- Write and illustrate at least ten examples from an ABC of Adverbs, e.g. *angrily, brightly, carefully,* etc. Use a dictionary for help.◆◆

- Write lists of adverbs related to particular actions, and use some of them in sentences.◆◆

- Set an adverb spelling test for the rest of the class that covers all the spelling patterns discussed in the whole-class session.◆◆◆

REFLECTING: *plenary*

- Share and discuss the adverb ABCs, commenting on interesting words and spellings.

- Carry out and mark the adverb spelling test. Which adverbs pose particular difficulties? Discuss strategies for remembering those tricky spellings. Which strategies do the children think would be most effective? Why?

Resources

Reading book

Practice PCM 29

Dictionary

Practice PCM 30

ASSESSMENT

- Identify common adverbs with the *-ly* suffix and apply related spelling patterns accurately.
- Explore the function of adverbs in sentences and use them accurately.

Adverbs

2/2

Focus
Sentence level
Grammar: using adverbs
T1/S4

Learning objectives
- to explore adverb use through moving and substitution
- to use adverbs with greater discrimination in writing

TEACHING: *whole-class introduction*

Resources

- Write up a simple sentence, e.g. *Dipika walked to school; Kelvin laughed at the joke.* Ask the children to provide more information by adding an adverb to each sentence. What adverbs could they use? Brainstorm a list of possibilities, drawing on ideas from the previous session. Say and write out the new sentences.

- Use the sentences created by the children to show where in the sentence an adverb could be added. Explain that there are usually several options for this: *Dipika walked slowly to school; Dipika walked to school slowly; Dipika slowly walked to school;* even *Slowly, Dipika walked to school.*

- **Shared text:** read out the Big Book page. Ask the children to try the following:
  - Substitute different adverbs for those used in the text. How do these changes affect the meaning of the story?
  - Consider possibilities for changing the position of the adverb in the sentence. Does this affect the meaning?

  Big Book page 11

- Shared writing: together, compose the next episode in this story, paying special attention to the way in which adverbs could be used to make the text much more detailed and vivid.

Adverbs

DEVELOPING: *group activities*

- Create new adverbs to fill the gaps in the sentences about traditional tales.◆

Practice PCM 31

- Examine a recent piece of creative writing. Have adverbs been used? How? Could more adverbs be used, or better use made of ones that have been included? If appropriate, revise the writing accordingly.◆◆

Dictionary Thesaurus

- Rewrite the next episode of the ghost story, using adverbs to make it more vivid and interesting.◆◆

Textbook page 23

- Write the beginning of a short ghost story, using as many interesting adverbs as possible. Use a dictionary and thesaurus for help.◆◆

Dictionary Thesaurus

- Use ideas about two very different children to write descriptions of their activities, using different adverbs to describe each of their actions.◆◆◆

Textbook page 24

REFLECTING: *plenary*

- Share examples of the use of adverbs in their own writing.

- Read aloud the ghost story episodes they have written; read through again, this time identifying the adverbs (the children could put their hands up when they hear one) and discuss their effect.

ASSESSMENT
- Recognise the effects of moving and substituting adverbs in sentences.
- Use adverbs effectively and with discrimination in creative writing.

Adjectives

Focus
Sentence level
Grammar: revision of adjectives
T2/S1, revision

Learning objectives
- to recognise adjectives and use the term *adjective* appropriately
- to recognise the impact of adjectives in writing of various kinds

TEACHING: *whole-class introduction*

Resources

- Check on the children's understanding of the word *adjective* as a *describing word*. Ask them to suggest as many adjectives as possible in three minutes. Write up each adjective as it is suggested. If the children have difficulty with this, suggest that they look at specific objects around the classroom and describe them, e.g. *bright light, sharp pencil, messy floor.*

- **Shared text:** read an extract from a story and/or a poem from the Anthology (or a known reading book), but omit the adjectives. Discuss how this changes the text, e.g. makes it less interesting. Explore how adjectives can be used in poems to add to the expression and impact.

    Anthology

- Discuss collecting and classifying adjectives, e.g. *colour, size, age.* You could begin a class collection or database of adjectives.

- Play the Adjectives Game: select an object in the classroom and give the children adjectives to describe it, e.g.:
  - *silver, shiny, pointy, cold* (*scissors*)
  - *big, flat, wooden, square* (*table*).

  The children should put up their hands when they guess the correct answer. The child that answers correctly then describes an object of their choice, and so on.

Adjectives

DEVELOPING: *group activities*

Resources

- Carry on playing the Adjectives Game. Write a list of all the adjectives that are used.◆

- Identify the adjectives in the text. Then rewrite the text using different adjectives.◆

  Practice PCM 32

- Cut out some photographs of the following from magazines: cars, holidays, footballers, bands, television or film stars. Stick these on to some poster-sized paper and then write some text underneath that includes as many adjectives as possible.◆◆

  Magazines

- Select a reading book and list examples of interesting or unusual adjectives.◆◆

  Reading book

- Imagine the class is going to put on an Adjective Exhibition in a few weeks' time. As a group, decide what kinds of adjectives could be collected, e.g. of colour, size. Present them for display, using examples in sentences.◆◆◆

  ICT

REFLECTING: *plenary*

- Read an extract from a reading book that illustrates the writer's skill in using adjectives.

- Share and discuss the ideas for an Adjective Exhibition.

Homework

- Find the adjectives in the poem. Then think of some more adjectives and use them to write a new poem.◆◆

  Homework PCM 14

ASSESSMENT
- Recognise and use a range of adjectives in reading and writing.
- Use the term *adjective* appropriately.

Adjectives

2/3

Focus
Sentence level
Grammar: comparative
and superlative adjectives
T2/S1

Learning objectives
- to examine comparative and superlative adjectives
- to construct adjectival phrases

TEACHING: *whole-class introduction*

Resources

- Recap on basic knowledge of adjectives, then introduce the idea of the three adjective forms:
    - *nominative* – the basic adjective: *tall*
    - *comparative* – used to compare two things, adding *-er: taller*
    - *superlative* – used to show the best or worst of three or more things, adding *-est: tallest.*

- **Shared text:** use the shared text to identify and discuss examples of nominative, comparative and superlative adjectives. Write up *tall-taller-tallest* and ask the children to suggest sentences in which they might be used, e.g. *The boy was tall, his brother was taller, but their father was tallest of all.*

Shared text

- Introduce the idea that not all adjectives add *-er* or *-est*: sometimes *more* or *less* is used for the comparative, and *most* or *least* for the superlative. This is often for longer adjectives, e.g. *This flower is more beautiful than that one, but those are the most beautiful.* Mention that some adjectives are exceptions, e.g. *good-better-best; bad-worse-worst.*

- Stress that adjectives should be used carefully in writing to add interest to stories and poems. Introduce more complex adjective forms and adjectival phrases, using examples, e.g. *Rudolph the <u>red-nosed</u> Reindeer; It was the <u>most red-hot roaring</u> fire she had ever seen; I looked at the beach with the <u>fine white</u> sand.*

Reading books

78

Adjectives

DEVELOPING: *group activities*

- Locate adjectives in a text and write them in a list, then change them for more suitable and interesting examples.◆

- Use a known reading book to locate and list a selection of adjectival phrases. Prepare to present them to the rest of the class.◆◆

- As a group, write a descriptive menu for a five-course meal. Build in some choice – and at least five examples of comparatives and superlatives!◆◆

- Devise a poster for the classroom wall that will remind children of the most important points about adjectives. Include plenty of examples.◆◆

- Take a short piece from an information text or a poem and swap five adjectives with adjectives of their choice. Try to make the piece retain some meaning. Ask another group to identify the substituted adjectives.◆◆◆

REFLECTING: *plenary*

- Begin a class collection or word bank of regular and irregular comparatives and superlatives.

- Discuss how adjectives with few syllables usually add *-er* and *est*, but longer adjectives usually use *most*, *least*, etc.

Resources

Textbook page 25

Reading books

ICT

Information books
Poetry books

ASSESSMENT
- Understand and use comparative and superlative adjectives effectively.
- Recognise and construct adjectival phrases.

Adjectives

3/3

Focus
Sentence level
Grammar: adjectives of intensity
T2/S1

Learning objectives
- to recognise how adjectives can suggest different levels of intensity
- to relate these to suffixes and adverbs

TEACHING: *whole-class introduction*

Resources

- Introduce the idea of adjectives of intensity, e.g. *hot* and *cold* are two opposites, but there are other descriptions in between, e.g. *warm, cool, chilly*. Discuss how these could make writing more interesting.

- Recap previous work on comparatives and superlatives and explain how these can also be used to form adjectives of intensity, e.g. *tall-taller-tallest*; *beautiful-more beautiful-most beautiful*. Discuss how some adverbs could be used also, e.g. *very still*.

- Choose four groups. Give each group an envelope. Each envelope should contain a different set of related adjectives on separate cards:
  - *hot, warm, lukewarm, cool, chilly, cold*
  - *gigantic, enormous, large, medium, small, tiny*
  - *gorgeous, beautiful, pretty, repulsive, unattractive, ugly*
  - *rapid, fast, swift, quick, steady, slow.*

  The group's task is to put the adjectives in order of intensity, starting with the most intense (hottest, biggest, etc). Share each group's order and talk about how adjectives can suggest shades of meaning.

- **Shared text:** introduce the children to the page from Dawn's school report. Show how it can be made better (or worse) by using the words in the box. (Answers: *fantastic, much better, dreadful, terrible, excellent, outstanding.*)

Big Book page 12

Adjectives

DEVELOPING: *group activities*

- Write an imaginary school report, using the Big Book page as a model. Include as many adjectives of intensity as possible, e.g. *This is Carl's best year at this school!*◆

- Rewrite groups of adjectives in order, then write a new list.◆

- Find three advertisements for different makes of the same thing e.g. computers, cars, chocolate. Write a sentence in each case that compares them and includes adjectives of intensity. For example, *X chocolate is sweeter than Y.*◆◆

- Choose a favourite holiday venue. Illustrate it and, in at least five sentences, describe its best features. Use at least six adjectives or adjectival phrases.◆◆

- Write the beginning of a short story or poem. Use as many adjectives as possible that use adverbs such as *more, most* and *very.*◆◆◆

Resources

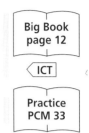

Big Book page 12

ICT

Practice PCM 33

Magazines

REFLECTING: *plenary*

- Share the imaginary school reports. Which do the children like best?

- Share the advertisements, the holiday venue descriptions and the results of the adjective investigation. Discuss how the adjectives could be put into a class collection or database.

ASSESSMENT
- Recognise that adjectives have various shades of meaning.
- Use adjectives with suffixes and adverbs to indicate degrees of intensity.

Sentences

Focus	Learning objectives
Sentence level Grammar: word order T2/S3	• to recognise how word order in sentences affects meaning • to apply this understanding to writing

TEACHING: *whole-class introduction*

Resources

- **Shared text:** use the shared text to focus on the idea of the order of words in sentences. Stress that how the words are organised is crucial to the meaning being properly understood. Focus on examples.

  Shared text

- Write up sentences with word order problems that give an unintended, comical meaning:
  For Sale – A pair of green children's boots
  Wanted – A table for four people with drawers.

- Ask: *What is the problem with these sentences? How could they be written to make the meaning clear?* Focus on rearranging words (*A table with drawers for four people*), though other changes could be considered, too (*A pair of green boots for a child*). (Reinforce if necessary by reordering nonsense sentences, e.g. *Always walk I school to.*)

- Move on to the idea that changes in word order do not always result in a change in meaning: they just give us different ways of saying the same thing. Illustrate this by writing up a sentence with a prepositional phrase at the beginning, e.g. *On Fridays we have fish and chips for tea*, and rewriting with the prepositional phrase at the end: *We have fish and chips for tea on Fridays.* Ask: *Is the meaning different?* Consolidate by shifting the order of words in similar sentences, e.g. from the children's own writing.

Sentences

DEVELOPING: *group activities*

- Arrange muddled parts of a sentence so that they make sense. Consider alternative ways of doing this.◆

- Reorder the words in five sentences, then write five new sentences, focusing on word order.◆◆

- Complete sentences where only the beginning, middle or end is given.◆◆

- In pairs, create a word order game: write a simple sentence, with each word on a separate card or slip of paper. Challenge your partner to put the sentence in the correct order!◆◆

- Give the group five prepositional phrases, e.g. *round the corner, on the wall, after tea, before bed, next to the school*. Ask the children to use each phrase at the beginning and then at the end of a sentence. ◆◆◆

Resources

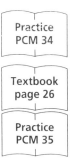

REFLECTING: *plenary*

- Share and discuss the group activities, contributing and writing up some examples. What are the alternatives? What works well? What does not work so well? What other changes sometimes have to be made if you change the order of words in a sentence?

Homework

- Rearrange the word order of the sentences so that they make sense.◆◆

ASSESSMENT
- Recognise the significance of word order in sentences.
- Investigate changing word order and retaining meaning.

Sentences

2/3

Focus
Sentence level
Grammar: connectives
T2/S4, T3/S4

Learning objectives
- to recognise how connectives are used to join separate clauses
- to use conjunctions to join ideas in sentences

TEACHING: *whole-class introduction*

Resources

- **Shared text:** recap previous work on conjunctions, e.g. *and, then, while, but, if, so, because* and illustrate with examples from the shared text.

    Shared text

- Consolidate this by writing up two sentences that could be joined into one using the conjunction *because*, i.e. the second sentence explains the situation described in the first:
    - *Shilpa did not come to school today. She has a cold.*
    - *The road is closed. A lorry spilt its load of logs.*

  Use the term *conjunction* to describe this type of word, and stress its function in linking ideas.

- Demonstrate the use of two other common conjunctions:
    - ***but*** (for linking opposing ideas). Making excuses is a good context for this, e.g. *I'd like to help you but ...*
    - ***so*** (for drawing out the consequences of an action or situation) e.g. *I had a bad cold so ...*

  Compose sentences using these two conjunctions. Extend, if appropriate, to cover other conjunctions, e.g. *or, when, if, unless, until, although.*

- Introduce the idea that conjunctions and other 'connectives' are a useful way to structure an argument. For example, adverbs, adverbial phrases and conjunctions can all be used: *if ... then; on the other hand ...; finally; clearly.*

Sentences

DEVELOPING: *group activities*

Resources

- Complete sentences using the conjunctions *but, so, and, because.*◆

  Practice PCM 36

- Use conjunctions *but, so, and, because* to join sentences; write own sentences using *but* and *because*.

  Textbook page 27

- Write a list of amusing and unlikely excuses, using the conjunction *but*, and/or a list of amusing and unlikely explanations, using the conjunction *because*.

- Look at a known reading book. What connectives have been used? Prepare to share examples with the rest of the class of how conjunctions and adverbs have been used to link ideas and structure an argument or a set of ideas, e.g. *finally, clearly.*◆◆

  Reading book

- Use a wider range of connectives in the middle and at the beginning of sentences.◆◆◆

  Practice PCM 37

REFLECTING: *plenary*

- Take each conjunction in turn; share and discuss some of the sentences they have written.

- Expand on the idea of connectives and clarify that they are a range of expressions (including conjunctions) for use in structuring an argument or a set of ideas. Share some examples.

Homework

- Join the sentences using the appropriate conjunction. Complete the remaining sentences to make sense.◆◆

  Homework PCM 16

ASSESSMENT
- Use a range of conjunctions in sentences.
- Understand and use connectives to structure arguments and ideas.

Sentences

3/3

Focus
Sentence level
Grammar: sentence transformations
T3/S3

Learning objectives
- to explore transforming sentences, e.g. statements to questions
- to recognise how this changes sentence grammar and punctuation

TEACHING: *whole-class introduction*

Resources

- **Shared text:** use the shared text to recap the difference between statements and questions, e.g. punctuation (statements – full stops; questions – question marks), grammar (questions often start with a question word, e.g. *who, what, why*).

  Shared text

- Write up a statement that can easily be changed into a question, e.g. *You enjoy making mud pies.* Invite the children to think of all the different ways the statement could be made into a question.
  - *Do you enjoy …?*   – *Are you enjoying …?*
  - *You enjoy …, don't you?*   – *Why do you enjoy …?*

- Discuss the changes that have been necessary to change the statement into each of the question forms, such as adding additional words, changing word order, tense and punctuation. Point out how tone of voice changes when a question is asked.

- Now write up a statement, e.g. *I want you to put your hands on your head.* Invite the children to change the statement into a command – *Put your hands on your head.* Discuss word changes that have been necessary (including deleting some words) and punctuation (e.g. an exclamation mark can add emphasis: *Put your hands on your head!*).

- Explore how statements, questions and commands can be made negative, e.g. by adding *don't* or *do not*.

Sentences

DEVELOPING: *group activities*

- Correct statements, questions and exclamations, focusing on word order and punctuation, then write two new questions.◆

- Read part of a playscript, then answer questions about transforming some of the sentences, including negatives.◆◆

- Write an imaginary interview (using question and answer form) about someone you know a lot about. Focus on correct grammar and punctuation.◆◆

- Prepare a short presentation for the plenary, to explain how the grammar of a sentence alters when the sentence type is altered. Mention word order, tense, punctuation, adding/deleting words. Include some examples.◆◆◆

- Write a sentence transformation quiz: create some statements, questions and exclamations, then mix them up and challenge a partner to sort them out!◆◆◆

Resources

Practice
PCM 38

Textbook
pages 28-29

ICT

REFLECTING: *plenary*

- Present the explanation about changing sentence types. Is it clear and helpful? Does anything else need to be explained?

- Play the sentence transformation quiz, using a range of mixed-up statements, questions and exclamations.

ASSESSMENT
- Recognise that sentences can be transformed to different forms.
- Understand how this alters the grammar and punctuation of a sentence.

Grammar revision

1/2

Focus
Sentence level
Grammar: sense and
accuracy
T1/S1

Learning objectives
- to reinforce awareness of grammatical coherence and agreement
- to apply grammatical understanding to writing

TEACHING: *whole-class introduction*

Resources

- **Shared text:** use the shared text to recap basic knowledge of parts of speech. Ask the children to find examples of nouns, pronouns, verbs, adjectives and adverbs.

  Shared text

- Challenge the children: what is the shortest sentence they can write? Discuss the fact that most sentences have a noun and verb e.g. *Dogs bark*.

- Recap on work from Stage 3 on grammatical agreement. Remind the children that the parts of speech in a sentence have to *agree* with one another for the sentence to make sense:
  - *He are a tall boy* (*he* is singular, so the verb should be *is*).
  - *They is very noisy children* (*they* is plural, so the verb should be *are*).
  Explore this further with more complex examples: *He are a tall girl* (in this case, the pronoun, verb and noun all need to agree).

- Focus on the idea of sense and emphasise that all sentences need to make sense. Again, use incorrect examples, e.g. *The bit baby dog the girl*. Stress that the problem here is word order.

- Remind the children of the three-point grammar 'code' introduced at Stage 3: *Does it make sense? Is it correct? Is it interesting?*

Grammar revision

DEVELOPING: *group activities*

Resources

- Write a short report entitled 'Yesterday in School'. Focus on grammatical sense and accuracy and use the three-point 'code'. ◆

- Use the words in the different columns to write a match report, then check the report for grammatical sense and accuracy. ◆◆

  Textbook pages 30-31

- Look back at a recent piece of written work and check it for grammatical sense and accuracy. Redraft the work where necessary to improve it. ◆◆

  Recent work

- In pairs, follow on from the whole-class session by writing five incorrect sentences. Then swap with a partner and write each sentence correctly. ◆◆

- Design and produce a poster or leaflet that explains nouns, pronouns, verbs, agreement, and how to check for grammatical sense and accuracy in writing. ◆◆◆

  ICT

REFLECTING: *plenary*

- Share and discuss writing done in the group activity session. Present examples of grammatically correct sentences.

- Discuss the explanatory poster/leaflet. Is it clear and helpful? Does anything need to be added?

Homework

- Choose the correct verb forms for the sentences. ◆

  Homework PCM 17

ASSESSMENT
- Apply an understanding of grammar to writing.
- Identify and correct grammatical inaccuracies in writing.

Grammar revision

2/2

Focus
Sentence level
Grammar: changing words
T3/S1

Learning objectives
- to recognise that some words can be changed in various ways
- to use this understanding in the recognition of parts of speech

TEACHING: *whole-class introduction*

Resources

- **Shared text:** use the shared text to recap the definitions of *verb* a (*'doing'/'being' word*), *noun* (*the name of a person, place or thing*), and *adjective* (*a describing word*).

  Shared text

- Write up two verbs (e.g. *play, run*), two nouns (e.g. *house, bird*) and two adjectives (e.g. *tall, heavy*). First, ask the children to identify which is which. Then challenge the children to see which words can be changed and how much. Tell them by 'change' you mean adding letters, or taking some away but without losing the same basic meaning. Give examples and refer to work covered in previous sessions:
  – verbs can change their tense: *played, ran*
  – nouns can become plural: *houses, birds*
  – adjectives can become comparative or superlative: *taller, heaviest.*

- Talk about other ways in which words can change, e.g. abbreviations (*'phone*); and contractions (*isn't*). Ask the children to suggest other examples of these kinds of changes.

- Point out that when a word can be changed in a particular way it helps to indicate whether it is a noun, verb or adjective. Use further examples from the shared text to illustrate the point.

Grammar revision

DEVELOPING: *group activities*

Resources

- Use a known reading book to find examples of nouns, verbs and adjectives that have been changed, e.g. nouns in the plural, verbs in different tenses, adjectives ending in *-er* and *-est*.◆

    Reading book

- Underline the verbs in the text. Then write the text again with the verbs changed, e.g. in a different tense.◆◆

    Practice PCM 39

- Look back at a recent piece of draft writing and ensure that nouns, verbs and adjectives have all been used correctly. Rewrite where necessary to correct any errors.◆◆

    Recent work

- Prepare a list of ways in which different words can be changed. Give examples.◆◆

- Design a reminder (that could be stuck to a pencil case or ruler) that summarises the way you can spot nouns, verbs and adjectives. Remember to keep the explanation as short and clear as possible!◆◆◆

    ICT

REFLECTING: *plenary*

- Share examples of nouns, verbs and adjectives found in reading books.

- Recap on the main ways in which words can change: plural nouns, endings of verbs, and comparative and superlative adjectives. Share and discuss examples from group work.

ASSESSMENT
- Recognise the main ways in which some words can be changed.
- Apply this understanding when locating and identifying parts of speech.

Commas in sentences

1/2

Focus
Sentence level
Punctuation: commas in speech
T1/S5

Learning objectives
- to recognise the use of commas in punctuating speech
- to apply this knowledge in writing

Resources

TEACHING: *whole-class introduction*

- Recap the basic functions of a comma: to mark a pause in a sentence or separate items in a list of items or points.

- **Shared text:** show the Big Book page, explaining that it is a conversation between a child and his grandmother. Read it out loud, and/or ask a pair of children to take a part each and read it.

- Draw attention to and highlight the use of commas. Emphasise how they help readers by indicating points in a sentence where they need to pause to make sense.

Big Book page 13

- Use examples in the text to illustrate the use of commas:
  - with people's names (*Haven't you grown, Billy; Billy, go and fetch my handbag*)
  - before question phrases at the end of sentences (*You still like them, don't you?*)
  - with common expressions at the beginning and end of sentences (*Yes, ...; Well, ...; ..., please*).

- In each case, prompt the children to find other examples in the text and ask them to suggest other similar sentences themselves independently. Write some of these sentences on the board, focusing on where the commas need to go.

Commas in sentences

DEVELOPING: *group activities*

- Find a text of dialogue in a story. Examine the use of commas. Prepare a group reading, paying special attention to punctuation and pauses.◆

- Use commas to punctuate their own examples of the kinds of things that grown-ups and children say to each other.◆◆

- Punctuate a text of dialogue in which commas are missing, and write a new passage of similar dialogue.◆◆

- Write a passage of dialogue for a story they are currently working on. Edit it to check that commas are used accurately and helpfully.◆◆

- Rewrite the beginning of a well-known story using only dialogue (or as a playscript). Edit it to check that commas are used accurately and helpfully.◆◆

Resources

Reading book

Textbook page 32

Practice PCM 40

ICT

Reading book

REFLECTING: *plenary*

- Read aloud the conversations they have found or written themselves, paying special attention to punctuation. Invite comments on whether they are easy to understand and whether they sound like people talking.

- Write a sentence of speech on the board, demonstrating and consolidating where the commas and other punctuation marks go.

ASSESSMENT
- Recognise how commas are used to help structure sentences.
- Apply this understanding when reading and writing speech.

Commas in sentences

Focus
Sentence level
Punctuation: commas in sentences
T1/S5, T2/S4

Learning objectives
- to explore the use of commas to show the grammatical structure of sentences
- to use commas effectively in writing

TEACHING: *whole-class introduction*

Resources

- **Shared text:** use the Big Book page to recap the basic purpose of commas in sentences: to separate two (or more) parts of a sentence and show where the reader should pause.

Big Book page 13

- Write up the following sentences:
  - *Tired after their long journey, the children stumbled up the steps to the massive wooden door.*
  - *Brushing the cobwebs aside, they stepped into the silent house.*
  - *They tiptoed across the rotting floorboards, with great care.*

  Together, read each sentence aloud and discuss how the comma helps by showing the reader where to pause and how the sentence works.

- Explain how each sentence consists of two parts:
  - one part conveying the main information
  - the other part providing additional secondary information. Identify and discuss other ways in which the same information could be conveyed, e.g. in two sentences: *They brushed the cobwebs aside. They stepped into the silent house.*

- Shared writing: write and punctuate sentences modelled on these examples. These could be linked to current fiction work, or to non-fiction topic work in another subject.

Commas in sentences

DEVELOPING: *group activities*

- Read a page or two from a story or information book currently in use. Identify and copy sentences in which commas are used. Be ready to present and explain how the commas help. ◆

- Punctuate a story in which commas are missing, then write the next episode in the story. ◆◆

- Write two-part sentences beginning with given words and phrases, using commas. ◆◆

- Examine a recent piece of writing. Have commas been used correctly and helpfully? If appropriate, revise the writing, making better use of commas. ◆◆

- Using a reading book or a non-fiction text, set sentence puzzles for a partner. Write out sentences without commas, and challenge a partner to put them back in the correct place. ◆◆◆

Resources

Story or information book

Practice PCM 41

Textbook page 33

Recent work

Reading book

REFLECTING: *plenary*

- Share and discuss examples of the use of commas.

- Discuss different ways in which they have punctuated the story extract. Where are commas necessary? Where are they a matter of choice?

Homework

- Add commas to sentences with lots of detail. Write further sentences to describe pets. ◆◆

Homework PCM 18

ASSESSMENT
- Identify the use of commas in the grammatical structure of sentences.
- Use commas appropriately in writing.

Apostrophes

1/1

Focus
Sentence level
Punctuation: possessive apostrophes
T2/S2

Learning objectives
- to recognise the use and function of the possessive apostrophe
- to begin to use the possessive apostrophe in writing

Resources

TEACHING: *whole-class introduction*

- **Shared text:** read the extract from *Flow* by Pippa Goodhart from the Big Book. Recap previous work on apostrophes for contraction and identify the examples in the text (e.g. *I'll, I'm*). Ask the children if they know the long version of *o'clock* (*of the clock*).

  Big Book page 14

- Introduce the idea that apostrophes can also be used to indicate possession: when something belongs to someone or something. Highlight the examples in the Big Book text, e.g. *Craig's family, Oliver's home*.

- Explain the basic rules for adding possessive apostrophes. Ask the children to suggest examples in each case and write them on the board:
  - singular nouns: add an apostrophe plus *s*, e.g. *the man's hat*
  - plural nouns ending in *s*: just add an apostrophe, e.g. *the doctors' surgery*
  - irregular plural nouns: like singular nouns, e.g. *the children's playground*.

- Shared writing: ensure that the children fully understand the difference between apostrophes for contraction and possession by together writing sentences that contain both forms, e.g. *Tomorrow, I'm going to see my cousin's new cat*.

- Recap the spelling session (page 38) and revise the difference between *its* (possessive – *the dog slipped its lead*) and *it's* (contraction – *it's hot today*).

Apostrophes

DEVELOPING: *group activities*

Note: use of apostrophes often causes particular difficulty and confusion, so work in this session should be extended and revisited for further practice and consolidation.

- Write five simple sentences where apostrophes are needed to show possession. ◆

- Use apostrophes to show possession and contraction. ◆◆

- Identify apostrophes of possession in a text. Use apostrophes of possession and contraction in sentences. Discuss the extent of their knowledge about punctuation. ◆◆

- Design and produce a classroom poster to show how to use apostrophes of contraction and possession. Remember to keep the details clear and concise, and include some examples. ◆◆◆

Resources

> Practice
> PCM 42

> Textbook
> pages 34-35

> ICT

REFLECTING: *plenary*

- Discuss the use of apostrophes for possession and contraction. Identify and share any interesting or unusual examples.

- Set a simple spelling test on some of the words used in the group activities.

Homework

- Add possessive apostrophes to sentences. ◆

> Homework
> PCM 19

ASSESSMENT
- Understand the difference between apostrophes for possession and contraction.
- Use possessive apostrophes accurately in writing.

Punctuation marks

1/2

Focus
Sentence level: basic punctuation
T1, 2, 3/revision

Learning objectives
- to revise capital letters, full stops, question marks and commas
- to use basic punctuation effectively in writing

TEACHING: *whole-class introduction*

Resources

- **Shared text:** use the shared text to point out various basic punctuation marks with which the children should be familiar: full stops, commas, question marks, capital letters at the beginning of sentences, and so on.

  Shared text

- Have ready an illustration, portrait or object for the children to describe orally. Invite single statements of description (for punctuation practice). Write some up on the blackboard and discuss the punctuation. Invite some longer sentences that will need commas (for punctuation practice).

- Discuss the punctuation of questions. Remind the children that question marks have their own built-in full stops and don't need additional ones.

- Tell the children that in their groups they are going to write a description of an imaginary animal called a *Grink*. It can be friendly or horrible, whatever they decide. Allow a five-minute discussion of the Grink's appearance, habits, food preferences, etc. What would it feel like if you touched one? What sounds does it make? Does it smell at all? Write up some ideas.

- Shared writing: together, write the beginning of the description of the Grink (just one or two sentences). Focus on using punctuation correctly.

Punctuation marks

Resources

DEVELOPING: *group activities*

Note: all groups should follow on from the whole-class activity by writing a description of a Grink. Differentiation will be by outcome, although the activity could be varied for different groups, as suggested below. Ask all groups to spend the last 3 minutes of writing time checking their work with particular attention to punctuation – full stops, question marks, capital letters, commas. If necessary, this could be used as an extended writing task outside the literacy hour.

- Write at least three sentences to describe the Grink, using the ideas on the board or a simple writing frame. Draw a picture to illustrate the description. ◆

- Write a detailed description of the Grink, using as many punctuation marks as possible. ◆◆

- Use a word-processor to produce a description of the Grink. Find and use the punctuation marks on the keyboard. ◆◆◆

ICT

REFLECTING: *plenary*

- Share work by reading each group description aloud.

- Discuss the punctuation that has been used. Does anything need to be added or corrected?

Homework

- Insert the full stops and capital letters so that the text makes sense. ◆

Homework
PCM 20

ASSESSMENT
- Recognise the functions of capital letters, full stops, question marks and commas.
- Use basic punctuation marks effectively in writing.

Punctuation marks

2/2

Focus
Sentence level
Punctuation: using
punctuation marks
T3/S2

Learning objectives
- to recognise punctuation marks: commas, colons, semi-colons, speech marks, dashes, hyphens
- to respond to them in reading

TEACHING: *whole-class introduction*

Resources

Big Book page 21

- **Shared text:** read the Big Book text and discuss the punctuation marks that it contains.

- Write up a list of punctuation marks and their basic functions, including the following. Identify which of these punctuation marks are used in the Big Book text, and which are not.

capital letters	– beginning of sentences; names (Gita, Diwali); titles (Mum)
full stops	– end stops
commas	– a pause in a sentence; in a list within speech marks to separate an additional comment or 'aside'
dashes	– for additions to main sentence
hyphens	– compound adjectives (ground-floor; blood-red)
apostrophes	– possession or contraction
speech marks	– direct speech
colon	– before lists
semi-colon	– to separate lengthy items in list; to indicate a pause in a sentence; longer than a comma

- The children may wish to discuss use of ellipses (three dots ...) to indicate when a piece of text has been omitted, or to show a 'tailing off' of text to suggest further details.

Punctuation marks

DEVELOPING: *group activities*

- Practise using various basic punctuation marks in context.◆

Practice PCM 43

- Use the punctuation list discussed with the whole class to find examples of punctuation marks not already discussed in detail. Prepare to present the examples to the rest of the class and show how they help the reader.◆◆

Reading books

- Read the extract from *The Angel of Nitshill Road* in the Textbook. (Don't answer the questions at the end.) Look at all the punctuation marks and decide why each one has been used.◆◆

Textbook page 28

- Add punctuation to a letter, then add speech marks to a conversation.◆◆

Practice PCM 44

- Imagine starting a new school, and describe the first day. Think about how punctuation will help the reader.◆◆◆

ICT

REFLECTING: *plenary*

- Emphasise that speech marks close *after* the final punctuation mark of the speech.

- Consolidate understanding of more complex punctuation such as colons and semi-colons.

Homework

- Identify the dialogue in the sentences and add speech marks correctly.◆◆

Homework PCM 21

ASSESSMENT
- Recognise and use a range of common punctuation marks.
- Respond to these marks when reading.

101

Authors

1/3

Focus
Text level
Fiction: author study
T1/T8

Learning objectives
- to find out more about a popular author
- to use this knowledge to move on to read more books

TEACHING: *whole-class introduction*

Resources

- Ask the children what books they have read by Roald Dahl. Remind them of the titles. Ask them if they can remember any characters from the books. What were the characters like? Can they remember any funny or exciting parts of the stories? What did they like or dislike about them?

- **Shared text:** read the extract in the Anthology from Chris Powling's biography. Ask the children what the extract tells them about Roald Dahl. How famous was he? Why do children like his stories? Why do some adults not like his stories? Explain that this extract comes from a *biography* – a book about Roald Dahl. Where else might they find out information about Roald Dahl?

  Anthology page 3

- Read the extract from *Boy* by Roald Dahl. Explain that this is from his *autobiography* – a book he wrote about his own life. What do they learn about Roald Dahl from his account of *The Great Mouse Plot*? How does it relate to Chris Powling's description of the risks and shocking bits in Dahl's books?

  Anthology pages 4-5

- If you have time, read the extract from *Matilda* in the Anthology. Explain to the children that Matilda is a very bright child who gets her own back on parents who are not very bright at all! Discuss the similarities between Matilda and the practical joke Roald Dahl himself played in *The Great Mouse Plot*.

  Anthology pages 13-15

Authors

DEVELOPING: *group activities*

- Write a short review of your favourite book by Roald Dahl. (Provide a writing frame for this: *My favourite book is … The best character is …. because ……… My favourite part of the book is ….because …, etc*).◆

- Design a poster to promote your favourite book by Roald Dahl.◆◆

- Prepare a short presentation for the class about Roald Dahl and the kind of books he wrote. Use the whole-class session and Anthology for ideas.◆◆

- Answer questions about the extract from *Boy* in the Anthology.◆◆◆

- Write a short comparison of the extracts from *Matilda* and *Boy* in the Anthology.◆◆◆

Resources

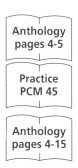

ICT

Anthology pages 4-5

Practice PCM 45

Anthology pages 4-15

REFLECTING: *plenary*

- Present ideas about Roald Dahl and the books he wrote.

- Share some of the reviews and ideas about Roald Dahl. Tell the children that Roald Dahl is so popular he even has his own museum in Aylesbury. He also has his own fan club. Its address is *The Roald Dahl Club, PO Box 3210, Sherborne, Dorset DT9 4YX*.

Homework

- Write a review of a favourite author.◆◆

Homework PCM 22

ASSESSMENT
- Investigate details of the life and work of Roald Dahl.
- Use this knowledge as the basis for reading more of his work.

Authors

2/3

Focus
Text level
Fiction: stories by a favourite writer
T2/T8; T3/T9

Learning objectives
- to read further stories or poems by a favourite writer
- to make comparisons and identify familiar features of the writer's work.

TEACHING: *whole-class introduction*

Resources

- Remind the children of the discussions they had about Roald Dahl in the last session. Children often like his work because he takes lots of risks and makes his characters do exciting things. He is also very good at creating tense, exciting moments. Can the children think of any such moments in his books?

- **Shared text:** read the extract from *The Magic Finger* in the Anthology, down to '*He sat up*'. Ask the children what they think might be wrong with Mr Gregg.

- Now read to the end of the extract. Talk about the ways Roald Dahl makes this incident tense and exciting. How does he build the extract up through little details? How does he keep us and the characters guessing by only revealing a little information at a time? (*He makes us wonder what has happened to Mr Gregg's hand. Mrs Gregg doesn't find out about herself until Mr Gregg tells her to look in the mirror.*)

Anthology pages 6-7

- If children can see a copy of the Anthology, point out that Roald Dahl uses very short sentences to describe Mr Gregg waking up and trying to use his hands. The short sentences help to make the incident quite tense. Read the first part of the extract again aloud.

- Ask the children if they can think of similar moments from any other Roald Dahl stories.

Authors

DEVELOPING: *group activities*

- Answer questions about *The Magic Finger* discussed in the whole-class session. ◆

- Prepare to read the extract from the Anthology aloud. Decide who will speak each line. Which lines might be loud? Which might be soft? ◆◆

- Read and answer the questions on the extract from *The BFG* in the Textbook. It also focuses on a tense moment. ◆◆

- Think of a tense or exciting moment in one of Roald Dahl's well-known stories (e.g. *Charlie and the Chocolate Factory*). Write a description of the moment and say why it is exciting. ◆◆

- Compare the extracts from *The Magic Finger* in the Anthology and *The BFG* in the Textbook. Write a short paragraph about each of them saying how Roald Dahl makes each moment very tense and exciting. ◆◆◆

Resources

Practice PCM 46

Anthology pages 6-7

Textbook pages 36-37

ICT

Anthology pages 6-7

Textbook page 36

REFLECTING: *plenary*

- Share and discuss the readings of the Anthology extract. How could they be improved?

- Discuss the similarities between the texts discussed and any other tense or exciting moments the children can think of in books they have read by Roald Dahl.

ASSESSMENT
- Select and read a range of material by the same author.
- Compare different texts and identify familiar features of the writer's work.

Authors

3/3

Focus
Text level
Fiction: range of texts
T3/T9,10

Learning objectives
- to introduce and explore work by Ted Hughes
- to describe and review own reading habits and widen reading experience

TEACHING: *whole-class introduction*

Resources

Resources: copies of *The Iron Man* and *The Iron Woman* by Ted Hughes (both Faber & Faber) if available. It would be useful if the children are familiar with the opening chapters of at least one of the books.

- **Shared text:** the Big Book text describes the first stirrings of the Iron Woman. Encourage the children to notice not only the massiveness suggested but also the pain that the creature is feeling.

  Big Book page 15

- Now read the extract from *The Iron Man* in the Anthology. Discuss the similarities and differences between this description and that of *The Iron Woman*.

  Anthology pages 8-9

- Point out that although *The Iron Woman* is described as a sequel to *The Iron Man*, it was published 25 years later. Both books have been described as modern fairy stories, both are a mixture of realism and magic, both have environmental themes, most obviously both involve a giant figure.

- Talk about why writers and other artists like to write or produce series of works around the same theme and/or characters. Discuss possible reasons for this, e.g. that the writer still has stories to tell about a particular place or topic; the characters have 'come to life' and the writer would like to explore them in another situation.

Authors

DEVELOPING: *group activities*

- Use the descriptions from the whole-class session to draw a labelled diagram of both/either the Iron Man and the Iron Woman, using the text.◆

- Write a short explanation of whether they like or dislike the extracts from *The Iron Man* and *The Iron Woman*. Describe the kind of books they like to read and give some examples.◆◆

- Read the text taken from *The Iron Man* that describes the first sighting of the giant figure. Discuss the similarities and differences between this description and that of the Iron Woman in the Big Book.◆◆

- Work out an oral reading of the text in the Big Book, marking the text to indicate how different elements should be read. Focus on both the Iron Woman's size and her pain.◆◆

- Write a description called *'The Best Read'*: describe the best book or story read recently, where they were (e.g. on holiday) and what they liked about it.◆◆◆

Resources

Anthology pages 8-10

ICT

Anthology pages 8-9

Big Book page 15

REFLECTING: *plenary*

- Encourage the children to reflect upon the two giant characters; their similarities and differences. If possible, make the complete texts available.

- Discuss how they could each widen their reading experience, e.g. by choosing a book they would not normally look at.

ASSESSMENT
- Compare related stories by a well-known author.
- Reflect on personal reading habits and identify ways to widen reading experience.

Playscripts

Focus

Text level
Fiction: narrative and playscripts
T1/T5

Learning objectives

- to prepare, read and perform playscripts
- to explore the differences between playscripts and stories

TEACHING: *whole-class introduction*

Resources

- **Shared text:** show the Big Book pages with parallel versions of an episode from *The Turbulent Term of Tyke Tiler*, from the original novel and the playscript adaptation. Quickly set the scene by explaining that the story is set in a school. Tyke's friend Danny has taken a ten-pound note from the teachers' tea money, and to keep Danny out of trouble, Tyke has taken the money from him and hidden it away. However, the headmaster suspects what is going on and has asked Tyke to come to his office.

- Read the two texts aloud. Prompt the children to examine the texts closely and to identify similarities and differences. Ask:
  - *How is the (tense) atmosphere conveyed? How do we find out about Tyke's feelings?*
  - *How is the dialogue presented? How do we know who is speaking?*

  Big Book page 16-17

- What is in the novel but not in the play? What is in the play but not in the novel? Who is telling the story in the novel? What is the effect of this? What is the significance of the formatting in the playscript (normal text, bold, italics)?

- Shared writing: together, rework a very short text from a story as a playscript; you could use a story which the children are currently sharing, a familiar fairy tale, or another text in the Big Book.

Playscripts

DEVELOPING: *group activities*

Resources

- Write a simple list of differences between playscripts and stories, using ideas from the whole-class session. ◆

- Look carefully at the two Big Book texts and describe how they each treat the following: what the headmaster is doing at the beginning of the scene, what he says, Tyke's answer, what Tyke is thinking, who is speaking. ◆◆

  Big Book pages 16-17

- Read another text from the novel of *The Turbulent Term of Tyke Tiler* and rework it as a playscript. ◆◆

  Textbook page 38

- Rework another short text (chosen from a familiar story or another page in the Big Book) as a playscript. ◆◆

  Reading book
  ICT

- Rework some or all of the scene in the Anthology as a story. ◆◆◆

  Anthology pages 11-12

REFLECTING: *plenary*

- Present and discuss ideas about the differences between playscripts and stories.

- Share reworkings of story episodes as plays and vice versa. Discuss problems and questions that arose in moving from one genre into another.

Homework

- Complete the playscript dialogue using the information provided. ◆◆◆

  Homework PCM 23-24

ASSESSMENT
- Prepare short readings and performances of playscripts.
- Recognise the main differences between playscripts and narrative.

Playscripts

2/3

Focus
Text level
Fiction: building scenes
T1/T6

Learning objectives
- to examine how play scenes are structured
- to investigate the build-up of a play scene

TEACHING: *whole-class introduction*

Resources

- **Shared text:** organise a group of children to read the scene from *The Turbulent Term of Tyke Tiler* in the Anthology to the rest of the class (there are seven speaking parts). Set the scene and read the stage directions yourself. (If possible, prepare and read this through with the children involved before the session.)

  Anthology pages 11-12

- Discuss the idea that scenes in a play are meant to move the story on, but they are also little stories or 'episodes' in themselves, with a beginning, a middle and an end.

- Lead a discussion about how the scene works, drawing the children's attention to:
  - how it begins and ends; the dramatic shape of the scene as a whole
  - what action is involved
  - interaction between the characters during the scene (identify the four main interactions: the Headmaster addresses the class; 'outcry' from children silenced by the teacher ('Sir'); dialogue between Tyke and Danny; Sir addresses the class)
  - entrances and exits during the scene.

  Anthology pages 11-12

- Record the structure of the scene, for example by using a time-line or listing the main events and interactions.

Playscripts

DEVELOPING: *group activities*

- Analyse and record the content and form of a play scene (This sheet could be used with the scene from *The Turbulent Term of Tyke Tiler* or a different play.)◆

- Answer questions about what happens in the scene in the Anthology and how this information is conveyed.◆◆

- Chart the development of a scene from a play of their own choice by writing a list of main events or a time-line.◆◆

- Choose a short episode from a familiar story. Rework the beginning or the ending of it as a play scene, focusing on the elements identified in the whole-class discussion.◆◆

- Draft a short scene based on dialogue between characters (e.g. two friends making up after an argument; children explaining misbehaviour to a teacher). Role play could be used to help.◆◆◆

REFLECTING: *plenary*

- Discuss what they have found out (from reading or writing) about the structuring of play scenes.

- Read out scenes they have written; work together to improve them, focusing on issues identified in discussion.

Resources

Practice PCM 47

Practice PCM 48

Anthology pages 11-12

ICT

Reading book

ASSESSMENT
- Recognise the main structural features of play scenes.
- Use this knowledge when responding to scenes and writing new scenes.

111

Playscripts

3/3

Focus
Text level
Fiction: using playscripts
T1/T5,13

Learning objectives
- to plan and write a complete play scene
- to develop skills of reading and performing playscripts

TEACHING: *whole-class introduction*

Resources

Big Book page 16

- **Shared text:** recap the main points about the features of playscripts from previous sessions, focusing on presentation of setting, character, action and dialogue. Reshow the Big Book extract to demonstrate this.

- Introduce the task to be started in this session. Explain that in the previous two sessions they have examined how play scenes work and written short scenes or beginnings or endings themselves. Now they are going to develop these short pieces into a whole scene.

- Recap the discussion of the structure of scenes from the second session, emphasising beginnings, building up the scene and endings. Encourage the children to keep the action in their scene very simple.

- Write up a 'scene planner' for the children to use during the group activities. Discuss each point:
  - *what is the setting?*
  - *who are the characters?*
  - *action – what happens? who speaks? what about?*
  - *directions – who enters and exits?*
  - *what happens at the beginning?*
  - *what happens in the middle?*
  - *what happens at the end?*

- Discuss some initial ideas for the kind of scenes that could be written.

Playscripts

DEVELOPING: *group activities*

Resources

Note: each of the activities below should use the 'scene planner' written up during the whole-class session. This activity could be used for extended writing across two or three sessions, focusing on structural elements and development of action. Include opportunities for ICT where possible, e.g. a word-processor, a tape recorder, or a camcorder if you have access to one.

- Rework a familiar short story or another known text as a play scene (link to work in session 1).◆

  Short story

- Write a scene including dialogue between at least two characters (link to work in session 2).◆◆

- Use an episode from the bullying story in the Anthology as the basis for a scene.◆◆◆

  Anthology pages 32-34

- Write a detailed scene that follows on from that in the Big Book. Identify clear setting, characters and plot outline.◆◆◆

  Textbook page 39

REFLECTING: *plenary*

- Read through and discuss the scenes at various stages during the process of planning and writing. Identify possibilities for development and improvement, focusing on issues discussed in the unit. Work together on these.

- Read and perform the finished playscripts to the rest of the class.

ASSESSMENT
- Plan, draft and write simple playscript scenes.
- Read aloud and perform the finished scenes.

Characters

1/3

Focus
Text level
Fiction: character details
T1/T1

Learning objectives
- to recognise how characters are built up from small details
- to explore how the reader responds to them

TEACHING: *whole-class introduction*

Resources

- **Shared text:** tell the children that this session will be about investigating descriptions of characters. Read the description of the Faun from *The Lion, the Witch and the Wardrobe* in the Anthology. Ask the children to tell you what the Faun looks like, what he is wearing and what he is carrying. Point out how carefully CS Lewis provides all of these details.

  Anthology page 16

- Now read the extract again. Ask the children to tell you which words or phrases suggest the Faun might be a comforting and nice creature (*neatly ... pleasant little face ... it looked just as if he had been doing his Christmas shopping*).

- Now read (or re-read following the Author session on Roald Dahl) the extract from *Matilda* in the Anthology. Ask the children what they think of Mr Wormwood. Is he very clever? Does Roald Dahl like him very much?

- Read the first paragraph again and ask the children to listen out for small details that tell us about Mr Wormwood's character. How does Roald Dahl describe Mr Wormwood's hat? What does Mr Wormwood think about his hat and his clothes? What does that tell us about Mr Wormwood? What does the whole incident tell us about Mr Wormwood? What do the children think of him now?

  Anthology pages 13-15

114

Characters

DEVELOPING: *group activities*

- Re-read the description of the Faun in the Anthology and draw a picture of it. Underneath, write a short paragraph.◆

- Make notes about Mr Wormwood. What kind of person is he? What details in the text show this? Use some ideas from the whole-class session.◆◆

- Read a detailed description from *Grandpa Chatterji* and answer questions about it.◆◆

- Find descriptions of characters in current reading books. Write a short note about the description saying whether they contain enough detail, say enough about the character and make the reader want to know more about the character.◆◆◆

- Compare the descriptions of the Faun from the whole-class session with the description of *Grandpa Chatterji* in the Textbook. How does each description tell us what the character looks like? What do we learn about the characters from the description of their appearances?◆◆◆

REFLECTING: *plenary*

- Discuss the similarities and differences between the character descriptions the children have read.

- Remind the children that we often learn about what a character's personality is like from detailed description of their appearance and actions.

Resources

Anthology page 16

Anthology pages 13-15

Textbook page 40

Reading books

ICT

Textbook page 40

ASSESSMENT
- Investigate how details can be used to build up characters.
- Explore how readers respond to these details.

Characters

2/3

Focus
Text level
Fiction: character sketches
T1/T2,11

Learning objectives
- respond in detail to fictional characters
- write character sketches, focusing on small details to evoke sympathy or dislike

TEACHING: *whole-class introduction*

Resources

- **Shared text:** re-read the description of the Faun used in the previous session (or focus on another character from a class story book). Remind the children of the work they did on character descriptions in the last session. Remind them that they learned about the Faun's character through details of his physical description and about Mr Wormwood's character through details of what he thought and did.

  Anthology page 16

- Tell the children you are now going to write your own character description of an imaginary creature like the Faun.

- First, brainstorm what the character might look like. Agree on the character's physical characteristics and write them on the board. Ask the children to suggest some adjectives to describe the creature, and add them to the list.

- Now tell the children you want to give hints as to what your character might be like (*fierce, kind, cruel,* etc). Agree on the character's personality. Then ask the children if they can add details to any of the physical features to give hints about the character's personality (*kind, warm eyes,* etc). Ask them to think carefully about small details to build up a picture.

- Explain that the character details built up here will be used during the group activities.

Characters

DEVELOPING: *group activities*

Resources

Note: each of the activities below should use the character details written up during the whole-class session. This activity could be used for extended writing across several sessions.

- Draw the character from the whole-class session. Write sentences or short paragraphs to describe the character's physical features and its personality.◆

- Write a character sketch based on the ideas from the whole-class session. Add any additional details where necessary and illustrate the description.◆◆

- In pairs, design a short 'character questionnaire' as a way of finding out extra details. Include questions such as *What is your name? Where do you come from? What are your habits?* Swap and complete the questionnaire to make detailed character sketches.◆◆◆

  ⟨ICT⟩

- Using the character sketch notes from the whole-class session, write a short story about meeting the mythical character. The story should contain the character description. It should then go on to explore what happens next.◆◆◆

REFLECTING: *plenary*

- Share and discuss the character descriptions and/or stories and show the pictures.

- Discuss what additional details could have been added to the character sketches to make them more interesting or exciting.

ASSESSMENT
- Offer detailed responses to fictional characters.
- Produce detailed character sketches.

Characters

3/3

Focus
Text level
Fiction: key characters
T1/T2

Learning objectives
- to understand and respond to fictional characters' feelings
- to empathise with characters, using information to predict actions

TEACHING: *whole-class introduction*

Resources

- **Shared text:** choose a big book or shared reading book that you have already started reading with the children. Read an extract to a point where one of the main characters is about to do something important or take some decisive action.

  Shared text

- Encourage the children to ask you questions as if you were the main character in the book. They should ask you about why you did things and how you felt, rather than for factual information.

- Ask for volunteers to attempt the same process, perhaps for a different character in the same book. The other children should ask them questions about what the character did and how they felt.

- Ask the children to imagine that they have been asked to advise the character about what to do next. Talk about what they would say.

- Re-read the last part of your shared text, stopping at a critical point where the character must decide what action to take. Ask the children to think about:
  - (a) what they would do next
  - (b) what their best friend would do
  - (c) what they think the character will do next.

  Shared text

Characters

DEVELOPING: *group activities*

Resources

- Following on from the whole-class session, write a description of what they would do next in the story, *or* what they think their best friend would do, *or* what they think the character would do.◆/◆◆

- Work with a partner. Prepare five questions to ask a character from a favourite reading book. Take turns to play the character and answer questions in role.◆◆

    Reading book

- Write a short letter as if you were the character in a favourite reading book, seeking advice on a problem.◆◆

    ICT

    Reading book

- Write a short letter to one of the characters in a favourite reading book, giving them advice on a problem and advising what to do next.◆◆

- Write the next part of the story discussed in the whole-class session. Think carefully about how the characters will act.◆◆◆

REFLECTING: *plenary*

- Discuss the question-and-answer activity and share some of the questions and responses.

- Listen to the problems outlined in the letters. Discuss possible solutions and replies.

Homework

- Answer questions about the characters in a text extract.◆◆

    Homework PCM 25

ASSESSMENT
- Understand, respond to and empathise with characters' feelings.
- Use information from the text to justify views and predict actions.

Structure and sequence

1/4

Focus
Text level
Fiction: chronology
T1/T3, 4

Learning objectives
- to develop understanding of how texts are organised into distinct phases
- to sequence events within a narrative and map how much time passes.

TEACHING: *whole-class introduction*

Resources

- **Shared text:** read part one of *The Mousehole Cat*. Finish the reading at '… *and caught fish for Mowzer's dinner.*' Talk about this as the introduction to a story. Ensure the children understand that the story is being told from Mowzer's point of view.

  Anthology pages 17-18

- Read the first sentence of part two of the story: '*Then one year there came a terrible winter*'. Explain this is where the author is complicating the story by setting a problem to be overcome. Ask the children to suggest what they think might happen.

  Anthology page 19

- Read the rest of page 19 in the Anthology and discuss how this part of the story is very different to the beginning. Encourage the children to recognise that the beginning of the story has a slow, relaxed, 'cosy' feel to it (the old rocking-chair, the '*beautiful golden glow*' of the fire). The middle of the story is very different: it describes one frightening event in lots of detail. Read the rest of the middle of the story and discuss what might happen.

  Anthology pages 19-22

- Read part three of the story and discuss how this phase is different to the middle phase. It is more calm and relaxed, like the beginning, and has more of a 'storyteller' feel ('*for when*'…). There is a big jump in time ('*and every year since that day …*'). Discuss how much time might have passed since the great storm. Look for evidence in the text.

  Anthology page 23

Structure and sequence

DEVELOPING: *group activities*

Resources

- With a partner, tell the events of the story in the correct sequence by drawing cartoons and writing a short description below each.◆

- Re-read part two of the story. List the sequence of events from the moment the boat leaves the harbour to the end of the storm.◆◆

Anthology pages 19-22

- Re-read the story. Examine the sequence of events involving the Great Storm-Cat and how Mowzer acts in response to him.◆◆

Textbook page 43

- Draw a simple time-line to show the events of the story. Discuss how much time might have passed between the beginning, middle and end, and write the main events on the time-line.◆◆◆

Anthology pages 17-23

- Read five events from part two of the story and sequence them. (*Answer: D, E, C, B, A*).◆◆◆

Practice PCM 49

REFLECTING: *plenary*

- Discuss the three sections of the story: beginning, middle and end. Explain how the middle could be split into two: complication (the storm) and resolution (the problem is solved and they arrive back safely). Draw a diagram or flow chart on the board to show the four phases: *introduction, complication, resolution, conclusion*.

- Question children to 'place' particular events within the different sections.

ASSESSMENT
- Investigate how stories are organised into distinct phases.
- Sequence events of a story and recognise how time passes.

Structure and sequence

2/4

Focus
Text level
Fiction: sequence of events
T1/T4

Learning objectives
- to consider the importance of an introduction to a story.
- to examine the climax and resolution in a text

TEACHING: *whole-class introduction*

Resources

- Discuss with children the nature of written stories. Authors rarely tell stories by simply making a list of events (*and then … and then.*) but organise the events so that they are interesting or perhaps tell us more about the characters.

- Explain that in a short story, where an author cannot use many words, not only do words have to be carefully used, but the organisation of the story is also very important. Then read *The Glass Cupboard*.

  Anthology pages 24-28

- **Shared text:** focus initially on the introduction to the story. Ask the children to identify what was special about the cupboard. Then encourage them to find examples of its special power. Finally, ask them to identify what special condition had to be fulfilled for the power to work.

  Big Book page 18

- Now ask the children to link the details in the introduction to the events of the story, e.g. the strange power of the cupboard made it a target for thieves. What other events in the story are made more interesting because they have been raised or suggested in the introduction? Collect their ideas in a table.

- Tell the children that the group activities will relate to the complication (middle) and resolution (end) of the story.

Structure and sequence

DEVELOPING: *group activities*

- Use a simple writing frame with the headings *Beginning, Middle* and *End*, to write a simple summary of *The Glass Cupboard*. ◆

- Closely examine part of the story, looking at each of the paragraphs in turn. Write a phrase or sentence that acts as a kind of heading for each paragraph, summing up the events. ◆◆

- Examine the climax and compare it with the conclusion to identify how they are different. ◆◆

- Experiment with the ending of the story by writing a short alternative, e.g. what might have happened if the thieves had not died? ◆◆

- Represent the events of the story diagrammatically, e.g. as a map of events, a spider diagram, flow chart, that fits the style of the story and also suggests the growing madness of the events described. ◆◆◆

Resources

Anthology
pages 24-28

Textbook
pages 41-42

ICT

REFLECTING: *plenary*

- Share the story again with the class. Discuss ideas for alternative endings.

- Discuss the plans, maps and diagrams of the story events. Which is clearest?

Homework

- List story events and then write a brief story. ◆◆

Homework
PCM 26

ASSESSMENT
- Explore the narrative order of a story.
- Investigate the importance of introductions, climaxes and conclusions to a story.

Structure and sequence

3/4

Focus
Text level
Fiction: planning stories
T1/T9,10

Learning objectives
- to consolidate understanding of story structure
- to explore different ways of planning stories

TEACHING: *whole-class introduction*

Resources

- **Shared text:** recap the story of *The Glass Cupboard*. Recall the main events: an object with a magical power is stolen, it gives the thieves great riches, but because they don't follow the rules, the cupboard brings first a kind of madness and then disaster.

> Anthology pages 24-28

- Explain how the story's events fall into a structure of *introduction, complication,* and *conclusion.* Help the children to place events into this broad structure using *introduction, complication* and *conclusion* as headings and listing events below them. From this list, underline how the main action and interest of the story lies within the middle *complication* section.

- Ask the children to debate why the story doesn't begin with the most important events. Can they explain what the introduction adds to the story, or what would be lost without it? Draw out through questioning features like a sense of place, a sense of rooting the events in a particular world, an understanding of the cupboard's magical powers without which the events would lose a lot of their point and interest. (The conclusion could be discussed in the same way, e.g. it links the story back to the beginning and neatly ties up all the loose ends).

- Explain that the structure of this story is a useful model to follow when planning their own stories.

Structure and sequence

DEVELOPING: *group activities*

Resources

Note: all of the activities below are designed as planning activities that will be followed up in the next session.

- Use a writing frame of *introduction-complication-conclusion* to plan a simple retelling of a well-known story, e.g. *Jack and the Beanstalk.*◆

- Develop the idea of an everyday object with strange, magical powers that could be used in a story. Brainstorm some details about the object and then plan the main events of the story in note form.◆◆

  ICT

- Use simple diagrams or a 'storyboard' technique to plan a story. Draw simple sketches to show the main events, and use captions to make things clear.◆◆

- Re-read the climax and conclusion of *The Glass Cupboard*. Then write brief planning notes for a new story as a sequel, e.g. with the King's new globe having magical powers.◆◆◆

  Anthology pages 27-28

REFLECTING: *plenary*

- Recap on the diagrammatic representation or mapping of the story. Ask the children to report back on their tasks, using the headings *introduction-complication-conclusion* to organise their contributions.

- Emphasise the value of knowing how stories are structured when planning their own writing. Encourage the use of a range of methods, e.g. brainstorming, notes, diagrams, storyboards.

ASSESSMENT
- Consolidate understanding of story structure.
- Use knowledge of story structure to plan new stories.

Structure and sequence

Focus
Text level
Fiction: writing stories
T1/T12,15

Learning objectives
- to write independently, using plans and drafts for support
- to develop use of paragraphs in story writing

TEACHING: *whole-class introduction*

Resources

- **Shared text:** briefly recall the main structural features of *The Glass Cupboard*, with reference to the planning model of *introduction-complication-conclusion*.

  Anthology pages 24-28

- Use some of the story plans produced in the previous session as the basis of a discussion. Explore some of the possibilities of each of the plans, initially focusing on the introduction. Re-read the opening paragraphs of *The Glass Cupboard*, down to '*a rich and powerful King*'. Highlight how the quality and range of ideas suggested in the introduction to a story opens out all sorts of possibilities for the rest of the story.

  Anthology page 24

- Shared writing: choose a plan from the previous session as the basis of this activity. Ask the children to agree on a 'magical object' to write about. Collect a few details and consider how the story might begin.

- Having agreed the first sentence and the object central to the story, encourage the children to suggest the next few sentences of the opening paragraph. Remind them of how the introduction needs to 'place' the object carefully, introduce its special or magical powers and also hint at some ideas which the story can pick up later.

- Remind the children of the need to organise the story into paragraphs, so that ideas are clear and the story is built up gradually (see also pages 140-141).

Structure and sequence

DEVELOPING: *group activities*

Note: all of the activities below are designed to build on the story plans produced in the previous session. They could be used for extended writing outside the literacy hour.

- Use the opening paragraph drafted in the whole-class session as the basis for a short story.◆

- Use plans from the previous session to write independently in paragraphs. If possible, link their own experience to situations in historical stories, e.g. a story in Elizabeth I's palace.◆◆

- Write an extended historical story, drawing on ideas from the previous session and the whole-class shared writing activity, and perhaps linking to history topic work. Use paragraphs consistently.◆◆◆

REFLECTING: *plenary*

- Ask the children to share their different ideas about the way the story develops from the agreed first paragraph. Reflect on how their plans relate to the finished stories and how they may have found it necessary to adapt their plans as they wrote their drafts.

- Help them to develop their understanding of the paragraph as a unit of connected sentences that develop ideas and move the story on.

Homework

- Finish off the story about the flooded house.◆◆

Resources

ICT

Homework PCM 27

ASSESSMENT
- Write extended stories independently, using plans as a tool.
- Use paragraphs to organise and sequence the narrative.

Settings

Focus

Text level
Fiction: details of settings
T1/T1; T2/T1, 9

Learning objectives

- to develop understanding of setting as an element in fiction
- to investigate settings and the details used to create them

TEACHING: *whole-class introduction*

Resources

Resources: a range of fiction with different settings, including realistic contemporary, fairy tale, fantasy and science fiction.

- **Shared text:** introduce the theme of the unit by reading the Big Book text. This is a very brief extract, but it is very effective in giving a picture of the setting through details. Ask the children for their ideas about the setting. Focus on details in the text, e.g. the child's 'name' (72B), '*windowless learning room*' (not 'classroom'), '*the bolts slam into place*', etc.

  Big Book page 19

- Encourage further ideas about the setting of this story. Ask: *Where does this story take place? How do we know? What do we know about this place? Is it real or imagined? What details can we build on, and what do we have to imagine for ourselves?*

- Ask the children to describe the setting of a story that they have recently read, considering the questions above. Develop the idea that some stories have real and recognisable settings while others have imagined settings, e.g. a future world, a fairy tale.

- Ask them to identify settings which are common in books for children of various ages (e.g. home, school, village, space, haunted houses, farms). What are the reasons for this? Develop the idea of writers having an 'audience' for their books.

Settings

DEVELOPING: *group activities*

Resources

- Write notes to describe the setting of a favourite book or kind of book. Illustrate it. ◆

- Follow on from the whole-class session by writing a description of the setting of a book or story read recently. ◆◆

  ICT

- Use a chart to carry out and record the results of a survey of the class (or year group) fiction collection. Write a short report, drawing some conclusions from the survey. What settings are represented? Are there any gaps? ◆◆

  Practice PCM 50

- Use the class fiction collection to find examples of stories with real and imagined settings. Organise and write labels for a small display of some of the books. ◆◆

  Reading books

- Identify and develop the settings of some very brief fiction extracts. ◆◆◆

  Textbook page 44

REFLECTING: *plenary*

- Share and discuss the findings about settings of books in the class fiction collection.

- Describe and present settings of favourite books.

Homework

- Read the extract and answer questions about the future world. Describe life in the future. ◆◆

  Homework PCM 28

ASSESSMENT
- Identify ways in which writers create imaginary worlds.
- Explore story settings by examining details in the text.

Settings

Focus
Text level
Fiction: influence of setting
T2/T2, 3

Learning objectives
- to explore the relationship between setting, character and plot in fiction
- to compare and contrast settings across a range of stories

TEACHING: *whole-class introduction*

Resources

- **Shared text:** read the three anthology texts in turn and discuss the settings with the children: traditional fairy tale, science fiction, modern/alternative fairy tale.

Anthology pages 29-31

- For each extract, ask the children:
  - *What characters do we meet in these kinds of settings?*
  - *What other characters are we likely/unlikely to meet?*
  - *What kinds of things are likely/unlikely to happen in these settings?*

  Brainstorm and list suggestions on the board.

- Discuss the differences between what an author can do if the setting is real and if the setting is imagined. Draw out the idea that if the setting is imagined the author can create any character and make anything happen – as long as it makes sense in that setting and is consistent.

- Introduce the idea that sometimes authors play around with the usual relationships, e.g. putting real human beings on another planet or into a fantasy or fairy tale world; putting a fairy tale character into the real world. Illustrate with examples from the Anthology (e.g. *Snow White in New York*), and from the class collection.

Anthology pages 29-31

Settings

DEVELOPING: *group activities*

Resources

- Match character and setting (e.g. princess to fairy tale setting) and vice versa. Create own matching characters and settings; choose one of these pairs, and write the first episode of a story.◆

  Practice PCM 51

- Read an extract from a modernised fairy tale. Explore what is unusual about it. What is different – the setting, the characters, the events, or all three? Write the next part of the story.◆◆

  Textbook page 45

- Choose one of the texts in the Anthology. Write the next episode of the story, focusing on fitting the character and plot with the setting.◆◆

  Anthology pages 29-31

- Rewrite the beginning of a well-known fairy tale, putting the characters and events in a realistic, contemporary setting.◆◆◆

  ICT

- Take the main character from one of the Anthology texts and put him or her in the setting of another. Rewrite the extract or write the next episode.◆◆◆

  Anthology pages 29-31

REFLECTING: *plenary*

- Share the story episodes they have written by reading them aloud.

- Discuss the relationships between setting and character. How are the character's actions and feelings affected by the setting? What happens if they are put in a different setting?

ASSESSMENT
- Develop understanding of how setting, character and plot are interrelated in stories.
- Experiment with changing these story elements in writing.

Settings

3/4

Focus
Text level
Fiction: story worlds
T2/T4

Learning objectives
- to explore the idea of story worlds
- to examine in detail how authors use language to create imaginary story worlds

TEACHING: *whole-class introduction*

Resources

- **Shared text:** use the Big Book page to introduce the idea of 'story worlds' – not just simple settings, but powerful descriptions where the reader is given a sense of whole worlds or environments, and all sorts of other things happening around the main characters. Discuss the Big Book page. Ask: *Where is this story set? What do we know about this story world? What words and phrases provide this information?* Highlight or list these.

- Remind the children of their work in the first session of this unit on the small but telling details in the description (e.g. the sound the door makes when it closes) and on the choice of exact and vivid words, especially adjectives.

Big Book page 19

- Shift the focus to the *mood* of the piece. How do the children think the writer wants them to feel about this place? What words and phrases convey this mood? Again, highlight or list these words and discuss their effect.

- Shared writing: together, write a short description of another imagined story world. For example, describe a kitchen or shop in the future world suggested by the school description in the Big Book. Focus the children's attention on word choice, on the description of detail, and on conveying mood.

Settings

DEVELOPING: *group activities*

Resources

- Continue the whole-class activity by writing a short description of a story world based on one of those in the Anthology, e.g. the weather and scenery on another planet. Draw a picture to illustrate it.◆

Anthology pages 29-31

- Plan, write and revise a description of the imagined world pictured, focusing on word choice, detail and mood.◆◆

Textbook page 46

- Write a description of a school of the future, but change the mood from the Big Book text, making it a welcoming and happy place.◆◆

ICT

- Read and examine in detail an extract that creates an imagined story world. Highlight significant words and phrases and annotate the text.◆◆

Practice PCM 52

- Write a commentary on one of the story worlds in the Anthology or one from another book. How does the writer use language to create this world? Be ready to share this information.◆◆◆

Reading book

REFLECTING: *plenary*

- Share and discuss the descriptions of story worlds they have written. Invite comments from others on detail, word choice and mood.

- Present and explain what they have found about how a writer creates a story world. Illustrate with quotations and close reference to the text.

ASSESSMENT
- Investigate the idea of story worlds through reading and examining various texts.
- Examine authors' use of language in creating story worlds.

Settings

Focus
Text level
Fiction: creating settings
T2/T10,12,13,14

Learning objectives
- to plan, draft and write a story set in an imagined world
- to make effective use of descriptive, expressive and figurative language

TEACHING: *whole-class introduction*

Resources

- **Shared text:** briefly recap on some of the shared texts from previous sessions, or choose another text.

  Shared text

- Introduce and outline the story-writing task for this session. Discuss story worlds they could create, asking the children to suggest possibilities. Brainstorm a list, including possibilities for other planets, future worlds and other fantasy worlds. Use the texts from previous sessions as models.

  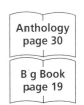

- Discuss ways of describing the story world, e.g. in an extended description, or sprinkling small bits of information through the story. Remind the children of what they have learned about writing descriptions of imagined worlds, especially the importance of word choice and detail, and the use of adjectives, descriptive and expressive language, etc.

- Discuss ways of planning and working on the story, e.g. they could work on their own or with others in their group, perhaps brainstorming ideas, creating the world and planning the story together and then writing a chapter each.

- Introduce the idea of writing notes as part of the planning and drafting process, then editing down the notes, removing less important elements and focusing on the really powerful and effective descriptive words.

Settings

DEVELOPING: *group activities*

Resources

Note: these activities are designed to prompt and support the children's story writing. Guide groups and individuals to those which you think they will find most useful and relevant, depending on their needs. The activities could be used for extended writing across two or three sessions.

- Work out the detail of the imagined story world, considering the senses of sight, hearing, touch and smell in turn.◆

  Practice PCM 53

- Start by drawing a picture of the imagined story world. Add annotations and additional information.◆◆

   ICT

- Write planning notes in response to questions about the story world.◆◆

   Practice PCM 54

- Write a story about Rosie and Rolf's visit to another planet, closely modelled on the extract in the Anthology, but adding a beginning and an ending.◆◆◆

   Anthology page 30

REFLECTING: *plenary*

- Share stories or story beginnings they have written, one type at a time, e.g. future worlds, fantasy worlds.

- Discuss the settings of these stories. What information does the writer provide about the imagined world? How clearly and vividly is language used to create this world?

ASSESSMENT
- Use various strategies to plan, draft and write stories in imagined story worlds.
- Use powerful and expressive language when describing the worlds.

Issues

Focus
Text level
Fiction: identifying issues
T3/T1

Learning objectives
- to identify social, moral or cultural issues in stories
- to develop understanding of the range of issues covered in stories

TEACHING: *whole-class introduction*

Resources

Resources: a collection of novels and short stories that raise issues, e.g. bullying, injustice, fears and overcoming them, jealousy.

- **Shared text:** read the first episode of the story in the Anthology. Ask the children what they think this story is about. Why do they think this? Prompt them, in their answers, to move from comments on what happens to identification of the main issue.

  Anthology page 32

- Extend the idea of issues in stories to others they have read. Ask the children to think of a favourite or recently-read story and say what they think it is about. Offer some other issues (e.g. fears and overcoming them, jealousy, sharing and selfishness) and ask if they know any stories about them.

- Compile a class list of issues in stories, e.g. by writing them up on the board or creating a simple display.

- Prompt the children to consider what issues are commonly found in stories for children (e.g. feeling jealous of a new baby; making and falling out with friends) and the reasons for this. What issues are not often found in children's books? Why not? Which ones would they like to be able to read stories about? Encourage them to relate this discussion to their own experiences (*Have you ever felt like that? Have you been in that situation?*).

Issues

DEVELOPING: *group activities*

Resources

- Survey stories in the class collection, identifying issues. Consider the findings and make generalisations or draw conclusions.◆

  Practice PCM 55

- Assemble a small collection of books about issues. Write a label for each and be prepared to present them to the rest of the class.◆

  Reading books

- Choose a book about a particular issue. Write brief notes explaining what the issue is and how it is worked out in the story. Select quotations that illustrate this, for a presentation to the rest of the class.◆◆

  Reading book

- Write a review of a favourite or recently-read book. Identify the issue, explain it clearly and describe how it is sorted out.◆◆

  Reading book

- Identify an issue that does not seem to be often dealt with in children's books. Write a letter to publishers to persuade them to produce books of this kind, explaining the reasons and giving them some ideas.◆◆◆

  ICT

REFLECTING: *plenary*

- Present the collection of books about issues and describe each one in turn.

- Present a book about a particular issue, explaining what the issue is and how it is handled. Read extracts to illustrate this.

ASSESSMENT
- Identify and discuss a range of issues in children's fiction.
- Explore specific issues and how they are dealt with in stories.

Issues

2/4

Focus
Text level
Fiction: exploring issues
T3/T8

Learning objectives
- to explore in detail how issues are handled in a story
- to write critically about an issue or dilemma raised in a story

TEACHING: *whole-class introduction*

Resources

- **Shared text:** read the first two episodes from the story about bullying in the Anthology. Prompt the children to share ideas about exactly what is going on:
  – *What is the problem faced by the two children who are being bullied?*
  – *What are their feelings and reactions?*
  – *What courses of action are open to them?*
  – *What might the consequences be?*
  – *What do you think they are going to do? Why?*
  Encourage the children to relate this story and the characters' actions to their own experiences.

  Anthology pages 32-33

- Read the rest of the story. Prompt and guide a discussion about what happens and how the writer handles the issue. Is this what they expected? Is it interesting, exciting, satisfying, convincing? Again, encourage the children to relate the story to their own experiences.

  Anthology page 34

- Shared writing: encourage the children to offer opinions on the story. Brainstorm a list of observations and ideas about the issue of bullying, the characters' dilemma, their course of action, what else they could have done and how the writer deals with the issue at the end of the story. Write up the children's ideas on the board, or ask a volunteer to do this on a sheet of paper. Identify and highlight the most important points.

Issues

DEVELOPING: *group activities*

- Imagine that the boys have still not decided what to do (i.e. the story up to the end of section two). Write a letter to them, explaining the possibilities and offering advice.◆

- Answer questions about the *Bullies* story, showing awareness of implicit meanings.◆◆

- Write a list of alternative choices for Tim and Greg, e.g. they could have carried on as they were, they could have tried to fight the bullies, and so on. What consequences would there have been for each?◆◆

- Agree or disagree with statements about the story, giving evidence from the text.◆◆

- Write an evaluation of the story, focusing on how the author handles the issue of bullying.◆◆◆

Resources

Anthology pages 32-33

Practice PCM 56

ICT

Practice PCM 57

Anthology pages 32-34

REFLECTING: *plenary*

- Use statements about the story from PCM 57 as the basis for a whole-class discussion. Ask the children who worked with this sheet to start off the discussion by presenting their view.

- Share the evaluations of the story, and invite comments. Do they agree/disagree? Why?

Homework

- Look at the cartoon strip about a burglary, write in the dialogue and answer the questions.◆◆

Homework PCM 29

ASSESSMENT
- Examine closely how issues are handled in a story.
- Respond critically to issues raised in a story, referring to the text.

Issues

3/4

Focus
Text level
Fiction: key moments
T3/T3,12

Learning objectives
- to identify key moments and alternative outcomes for the story
- to consider how paragraphs are used to organise stories

TEACHING: *whole-class introduction*

Resources

- **Shared text:** the children have already begun to identify and consider alternative courses of action and outcomes in the story. Develop this by re-reading the second section of the story up to the point where Tim finds his smashed lunchbox. Ask the children what else he and Greg might have done at this point. What might have happened as a result?

  Anthology page 33

- Ask the children to identify other key moments and turning points in the story, e.g. walking to school; when they meet the bullies for the first time that day; when they talk to Mr Silver in the empty classroom. Again, consider other ways in which the characters might have reacted and other turns of events.

- Ask the children what they think is the single most important moment in the story, the crisis point. (There should be agreement that this is the moment when Tim discovers that the bullies have smashed his lunchbox, decides that things have now gone too far, and that he will tell his teacher.) Re-read this episode. Discuss how the author builds up to this moment (e.g. Sebastian's silent bullying in the classroom) and resolves events following it.

  Anthology pages 32-34

- Discuss how the author's use of paragraphs is very important in the building-up of ideas. Refer to the text to show how each paragraph adds a new event or idea – even very short paragraphs.

Issues

DEVELOPING: *group activities*

- Read the three story sections again. Decide on a chapter title for each which sums up the main focus of the action. ◆

- Draw and annotate a time-line to chart the main events in the story. Use the paragraphs as 'markers' on the time-line. ◆◆

- Explore how the story is built up by answering questions about what happens. ◆◆

- Read a short turning-point moment from the story and consider the possible courses of action and their likely consequences. Continue the story, taking it in a different direction from that in the original story. Use paragraphs. ◆◆

- Brainstorm, plan and write a new, shocking ending for the story, e.g. Mr Silver does not believe Tim and Greg, and they end up being punished instead. How would this change your view of the characters and events of the original story? ◆◆◆

Resources

Anthology pages 32-34

Anthology pages 32-34

Practice PCM 58

Textbook page 47

ICT

REFLECTING: *plenary*

- Share chapter titles for the three sections of story. Do they capture the main action of the sections?

- Read alternative episodes and endings they have written. Are they believable? How do these outcomes change the way we feel about the characters?

ASSESSMENT
- Explore and experiment with key moments and endings of the story.
- Recognise how paragraphs and chapters are used to organise and build up ideas.

Issues

4/4

Focus
Text level
Fiction: extended story
T3/T11,13

Learning objectives
- to continue investigation of story structure
- to plan and write an extended story

TEACHING: *whole-class introduction*

Resources

- **Shared text:** re-read the *Bullies* story in full and explain to the children that this session will focus on them writing their own 'issues' story in chapters.

  Anthology pages 32-34

- Brainstorm possible subjects for this, drawing on the identification of issues in fiction from the first session in this unit (pages 136-137).

- Introduce the three planning sheets, explaining that they offer different ways of planning stories. (These could be written up on the board, or enlarged photocopies could be made on A3 sheets.)

- Demonstrate the use of each planning sheet by completing each one in relation to the story in the Anthology. (As well as supporting their own story planning, this gives the children another way of investigating the structure of the story they have been reading and working on.)

  Practice PCM 59-61

  1) Planning in chapters, with titles and notes on main events
  2) Planning by deciding on the different elements of the story
  3) Planning by tracing the plot line

- If appropriate, reassure the children that they can base their stories on ideas, characters and events from the story in the Anthology or others from the first session in this unit.

Issues

DEVELOPING: *group activities*

Note: the core story planning and writing activity is likely to take 2 or 3 sessions, perhaps more. The photocopiable materials below are designed to prompt and support the initial planning stages during the first of these sessions. Guide groups and individuals to those sheets that you think they will find most useful and relevant, depending on their needs, using ICT where possible. Stress the need to use clear paragraphs.

- Plan out a story in chapters, finding a title and making notes on the main event for each. (This could be extended beyond the three initial chapters, if necessary.) ◆

  Practice PCM 59

- Plan a story by deciding on the main elements: the issue, the setting, the characters, the problem, the solution. ◆◆

  Practice PCM 60

- Plan a story by developing the plot-line: the beginning, subsequent events, the turning point, the ending. ◆◆◆

  Practice PCM 61

REFLECTING: *plenary*

- Pause after the first session for children to share plans or opening chapters: does this look promising? Does it catch the reader's interest? Could the plans or drafts be modified in any way to improve them?

- Share the whole stories as they are completed. Discuss the issues and the way they are handled in each story. Focus on interesting, unusual or unexpected examples.

ASSESSMENT
- Use detailed plans as the basis for story writing.
- Write extended stories using chapters and paragraphs.

Resources

Stories from other cultures

1/3

Focus
Text level
Fiction: place and time
T3/T2

Learning objectives
- to focus on the elements of time and place in storytelling
- to explore cultural differences demonstrated in stories

TEACHING: *whole-class introduction*

Resources

- **Shared text:** read the extract from *Grace and Family* by Mary Hoffman from the Big Book. Briefly explain the background to this extract – Grace has travelled with her grandmother to visit her father, who lives in the Gambia.

  Big Book page 20

- Help the children to locate The Gambia in West Africa on a map or globe. Show them where Britain is in relation to The Gambia. Discuss the long journey Grace and Nana had made to get there. Have any of the children been on similar long journeys, e.g. for holidays?

- Discuss the differences in climate that are highlighted in the text: it is Easter, which is often cold and wet in Britain! Which words and details show us how very hot it is in The Gambia?

- What differences from Britain does Grace notice as she looks around her? If the children were painting a picture of the scene, which details would be important? What colours would they use?

  Big Book page 20

- How does Grace feel on her first visit to The Gambia? What evidence is there in the text to support this? (Notice the final exclamation mark, which suggests a sense of wonder, excitement, surprise, enjoyment, anticipation, etc.)

Stories from other cultures

DEVELOPING: *group activities*

Resources

- Reversing the cultural situation: imagine a first visit to Britain and write about expectations and observations of the visit, using a writing frame.◆

Practice PCM 62

- Write a list of the similarities and differences in the Big Book text between life in Britain and life in The Gambia. Prepare to present the list to the class.◆

Big Book page 20

- Write a letter from Grace to a friend in England, describing her visit to The Gambia.◆◆

ICT

- Write a new version of the Big Book text, but this time imagine that Grace lives in The Gambia and is visiting Britain for the first time. What differences would she see?◆◆

- Explore and analyse a text about a young girl in India.◆◆◆

Textbook pages 48-49

REFLECTING: *plenary*

- Share and discuss the list of similarities and differences between life in The Gambia and in Britain. What else could be added to the list?

- Share experiences of foreign travel and first impressions of other countries.

Homework

- Read the text about the Caribbean and answer the questions comparing it with Britain.◆◆

Homework PCM 30

ASSESSMENT
- Explore elements of time and place in stories from other cultures.
- Investigate cultural differences in fiction.

Stories from other cultures

2/3

Focus
Text level
Fiction: customs and
relationships
T3/T2

Learning objectives
- to investigate relationships between members of different cultures
- to examine similarities and differences between different cultural traditions

TEACHING: *whole-class introduction*

Resources

- Remind the children of Grace's visit to Africa and how different from Britain everything seemed when she first arrived there.

  Big Book page 20

- **Shared text:** introduce the extract from *Lights for Gita* by explaining that Gita and her family have only recently moved to Britain from New Delhi in India. Locate New Delhi on a map or globe, in relation to Britain. Briefly discuss Diwali, the Hindu festival of lights, then read the Big Book text.

  Big Book page 21

- Discuss what we learn about Diwali from this extract (festival of lights, parties, sweets, fireworks, stories, family traditions). Share any experiences the children have of Diwali and write up some of their ideas about the festival.

- Discuss the line *'How could this place ever be home?'* (paragraph 2). How different for Gita will Diwali be this year? Look for clues in the text, e.g. how *'warm and joyful'* Diwali had been last year.

- Briefly discuss the idea of *customs* of certain cultures: long-established traditions, habits and practices that are passed from one generation to the next, often linked to religion and involving the whole family. Examples in Britain might include Christmas, Easter, Eid, Passover, Hannukah, etc.

Stories from other cultures

DEVELOPING: *group activities*

- Read the short text about Diwali, then use the sheet as a starting-point for discussion.◆

- Use the class or school library to investigate as much as possible about Diwali, the Hindu festival of lights. Write a report on the findings for a wall display.◆◆

- Continue the activity from the whole-class session by listing as many different cultures and traditions as possible, finding examples in class books (fiction and non-fiction).◆◆

- Answer comprehension questions about making diyas, and sequence the stages of making them.◆◆

- Write a letter from Gita to her grandmother in India, explaining how she feels about the relationship with her family in India and the customs she is carrying on in Britain.◆◆◆

Resources

Anthology page 35

Practice PCM 63

Library books

Textbook pages 50-51

REFLECTING: *plenary*

- Share and discuss the findings about Diwali. What else could be added to the display?

- Read the letters to Gita's grandmother and discuss how Gita might feel about life in Britain and her Indian customs and relationships.

ASSESSMENT
- Investigate cultural traditions, with specific reference to the festival of Diwali.
- Explore family relationships in the context of different cultures and traditions.

147

Stories from other cultures

3/3

Focus
Text level
Fiction: themes
T3/T2

Learning objectives
- to explore the theme of cultural conflicts
- to investigate how cultural divides could best be bridged

TEACHING: *whole-class introduction*

Resources

- **Shared text:** read *Life for a young Asian girl* in the Anthology. Locate Nepal on a map or a globe and explain how the author of this text (Sangita) feels torn between two cultures – the traditions of her Nepalese family, and the very different customs and lifestyle of living in Britain.

Anthology page 36

- Ask the children what they think Sangita means when she says *'I don't know who I am, a Nepalese girl or an English girl.'* Draw out the idea that she is a bit of both – and her main problem is balancing her everyday life in Britain with her relationships at home with her family, and their customs.

- Discuss how Sangita's confusion as a Nepalese girl in Britain is similar to the other stories explored in this unit. For example, in *Grace and Family*, Grace visits the Gambia for the first time, and in *Lights for Gita*, Gita has to celebrate Diwali for the first time in cold and wet Britain.

- Discuss the idea that living with two different cultures and the confusion or unhappiness of the characters involved are *themes*. Refer to previous work on themes and discuss the meaning of the term.

- Discuss ways in which different cultures can work together. What could be done by families, schools, friends, media, etc? Invite the children to discuss their own experiences of sharing two cultures.

Stories from other cultures

DEVELOPING: *group activities*

Resources

- Follow on from the whole-class session by exploring how life might be different in a new country. (This could be used as a structured discussion sheet or as questions requiring personal written responses.) ◆/◆◆

  Practice PCM 64

- Re-read the Anthology text about Diwali and write some ideas about how people in one country could learn about the customs and traditions of another country. ◆◆

  Anthology page 35

- Brainstorm a list of ideas for how Sangita could make herself feel happy. Prepare to present the list to the rest of the class. ◆◆

  Anthology page 36

- Read another part of the story *Lights for Gita*, and answer questions about it. ◆◆

  Textbook page 52

- Think about the three stories discussed in this unit. Write a letter giving advice to a young child from a different culture coming to live in Britain. What information would be essential? What would be the most important advice for them? ◆◆◆

REFLECTING: *plenary*

- Share ideas for how Sangita could cope with her problems.

- Discuss what they could do as children to help build bridges between different cultures. Do they have any direct experience of this?

ASSESSMENT
- Explore cultural conflicts, with reference to specific texts.
- Suggest constructive ways of sharing two or more cultures, with reference to their own experience where possible.

149

Common themes in poetry

1/3

Focus
Text level
Poetry: examining poems
T1/T7

Learning objectives
- to examine a poem in detail
- to discuss personal responses and preferences

Resources

TEACHING: *whole-class introduction*

- Explain that the theme of the session is the sea. Ask the children to discuss its significance to them (e.g. holidays), or if they have never seen the sea, what they imagine it to be like. Talk about how the sea provides work for people (fishermen, merchant sailors) and that it can be a dangerous way of life.

- **Shared text:** together, read James Reeves' poem *The Sea* from the Big Book. Highlight the central image of the poem – that the sea is like a dog. Do they think this is a good comparison? Why?

- Re-read the poem to the class, giving special emphasis to the verbs. List the verbs on the board and ask the children to identify what part of speech they are. Remind the children of the basic definition of this part of speech (*a 'doing' or 'being' word*). Explain that the poet has chosen the verbs carefully to suggest the way that both dogs and the sea move.

Big Book page 22

- Ask the children to look carefully again at the poem and particularly at the verbs. Discuss and classify the verbs under headings, such as:
  - movement: *rolls, rocks, bounds*
  - other action: *gnaws, licking, play, lies*
  - sound: *moans, roars, snuffs, howls, hollos, snores.*

Point out how each of the verbs suggests the actions, movements or sounds of a dog, but also the sea.

Common themes in poetry

DEVELOPING: *group activities*

- Read the poem aloud, exploring how voices can be used to convey the different moods of the dog and sea. Use a tape recorder to experiment with different readings.◆

- Look at the list of verbs from *The Sea* compiled during the whole-class session. Use a dictionary to explain the meaning of each verb.◆◆

- Choose three verbs from the poem and explain how each fits the actions of a dog and the movement of the sea.◆◆

- Discuss personal preferences for this poem. Who in the group likes or dislikes the poem? Be sure to support opinions with evidence from the text, and prepare to present opinions to the class.◆◆

- Investigate two or three of the 'snapshots' or pictures in the poem, e.g. *'Hour upon hour he gnaws/The rumbling tumbling stones …'; 'With his head between his paws/ He lies on the sandy shores …'* What sort of sea is the poet describing in these pictures?◆◆◆

Resources

Big Book page 22

ICT

Dictionary

Practice PCM 65

Big Book page 22

REFLECTING: *plenary*

- Discuss personal opinions about the poem, using evidence from the text to support ideas.

- Present tape-recorded readings of the poem. How could they be improved?

ASSESSMENT
- Examine a poem in detail, with specific reference to the verbs.
- Generate responses to and opinions about a poem, with close reference to the text.

Common themes in poetry

2/3

Focus
Text level
Poetry: comparing and contrasting poems
T1/T7

Learning objectives
- to compare and contrast poems on similar themes
- to use form and language as a way of doing this

TEACHING: *whole-class introduction*

Resources

- **Shared text:** re-read *The Sea* and recap the work from the previous session. Introduce the idea of 'themes' in different poems: ideas treated in different ways or from a different point of view.

  Big Book page 22

- Discuss the different themes that could be drawn out of *The Sea*. Most obvious is the behaviour of the sea at different times, but this could be extended to the environment in general.

- Ask the children to suggest poems about the environment that they have read in anthologies. How are they similar to or different from *The Sea*?

- Introduce the idea of *comparing* (looking for similarities) and *contrasting* (looking for differences) poems. As an introduction to this idea, read the haiku at the top of page 27 in the Big Book. Ask the children to compare and contrast it with *The Sea*.

  Big Book page 27

- The haiku is obviously a very different poem to *The Sea*, so the children are most likely to spot the contrasts: the haiku is about birds, it is very short and compact, it contains only one verb ('*sitting*') and it focuses on only one feature of the birds. However, there are also points of comparison: e.g. both the haiku and *The Sea* relate to animals and the environment, and they both refer to the weather.

Common themes in poetry

DEVELOPING: *group activities*

Resources

- Read the haiku aloud, exploring how voices can be used to convey the mood of the poem. How is it different to *The Sea*? Use a tape recorder to experiment with different readings.◆

Big Book page 27

ICT

- Draw a picture for classroom display to go with each poem discussed in the whole-class session.◆

- Use poetry anthologies to research other poems about animals and/or the environment. Discuss how they are similar to or different from *The Sea*.◆◆

Poetry anthologies

- Use class books and anthologies to compile a list of other common themes in children's poems, e.g. school, families, feelings. Choose one theme and prepare two poems to present to the class.◆◆

Poetry anthologies

- Write a list of advantages and disadvantages for each type of poem: long, detailed descriptions with lots of verbs, and short, sharp, compact poems.◆◆◆

REFLECTING: *plenary*

- Discuss poems found that are similar to and different from *The Sea*. Use examples from each poem.

- Present the two poems on the selected theme. Which do the class prefer? Why?

Homework

- Compare and contrast two poems about birds.◆◆◆

Homework PCM 31

ASSESSMENT
- Recognise that poems on similar themes can both compare and contrast.
- Use the language and structure of poems to support ideas.

153

Common themes in poetry

3/3

Focus
Text level
Poetry: writing poetry
T1/T14

Learning objectives
- to write poems based on personal or imagined experience
- to link writing to poems read, e.g. language and structure

TEACHING: *whole-class introduction*

Resources

- **Shared text:** re-read *The Sea*. Encourage the children to recall how the poem is based around a central image or idea (that the sea is like a dog) and that Reeves has carefully chosen verbs to suggest the movement and actions of both the sea and a dog.

Big Book page 22

- Explain to the children that they are going to use this poem as a model for writing their own. The aim is to adopt the idea of writing about one thing as if it were another.

- Recap some of the group work from the previous session on finding a common theme – something everyone knows something about, or has experienced. Explain that the focus for this session will be on a particular part of the environment: the weather.

- Explain that weather has often been described in terms of other things (e.g. *it's raining cats and dogs*). Talk about some different weather conditions, e.g. rain, hail, sleet, snow, heatwave.

- Shared writing: ask the children to explore weather in human terms, e.g. if mist was a person what would he/she be like (e.g. *cool, pale, mysterious*)? Together, draft a few lines of a poem that describes the weather as if it was the person or object.

Common themes in poetry

DEVELOPING: *group activities*

Note: the following activities involve developing the whole-class shared writing by considering the children's choice of verbs and the sorts of 'pictures' they can suggest, just as James Reeves managed in his poem. This work could be extended across several sessions. Include ICT opportunities where possible.

- Think of a certain type of weather and a person, animal or thing to compare it to, e.g. a person and mist. Write a list of verbs that suggest the way that this thing moves or that describe actions that are characteristic of it. Then write a series of sentences using each of these verbs, e.g. *The mist glides like a dancer.* ◆

- Draft ideas about a set of weather conditions, using ideas from the activity sheet as support. ◆◆

- Convey the particular weather conditions in no more than 50 words, or 10 lines. Since they have so few words they must not waste any. Pay particular attention to verbs and use comparisons (e.g. *the mist is like a ghost*) to convey the nature of the weather. ◆◆◆

REFLECTING: *plenary*

- Listen to some drafts. Highlight particular moments of insight, interesting uses of language, and use of different techniques.

- Discuss ideas for further drafting, including integrating ideas from different groups, or focusing further on the use of verbs and comparisons.

Resources

Practice
PCM 66

ASSESSMENT
- Write poems that draw on personal or imagined experience.
- Use poems read as a model of language and structure.

Classic and modern poetry

Focus
Text level
Poetry: language
T2/T4, 5

Learning objectives
- to recognise how the language of poetry and prose differs
- to develop response to poetry, both oral and written

TEACHING: *whole-class introduction*

Resources

- Ask the children to imagine a wet day in October, and together, write a brief weather forecast for it, e.g. *Thursday will be wet and windy in the north, with rain moving south. Overnight it will be cloudy with high winds.*

- **Shared text:** read the modern poem *Take Two*. Then break the poem into smaller chunks for discussion:
  - '*A bruise of wind/fists the street*': discuss how these lines show the idea of strong, harsh winds. What do the words '*bruise*' and '*fists*' make the children think of (e.g. fighting, pain, bullies)?
  - '*a knuckle of rain/punches south*': this suggest more violent, rapid action.
  - '*The shutters bark/back and the moon/coughs discreetly*': shutters on windows are banging about in the wind, sounding like barking dogs, while quieter and softer wind noises sound like 'coughs'.
  - '*Night nibbles the dawn*': the night is coming to an end and light begins to spread across the sky.
  - '*The stars lose control*': this could just mean that the stars disappear as the sky becomes lighter, or it could suggest that the violent weather has been so strong that even the stars have been blown about!

Big Book page 23

- Discuss the differences between the poem and the weather forecast, e.g. the forecast uses plain language to be as clear, direct and straightforward as possible, while the poem uses figurative language to suggest many different ideas, thoughts and images.

Classic and modern poetry

DEVELOPING: *group activities*

Resources

- Choose one or two lines from *Take Two* in the Big Book and illustrate them. Think about the ideas discussed with the whole class and use these in the illustration.◆

Big Book page 23

- Prepare a group reading or tape recording of *Take Two* or another modern poem about the weather.◆◆

ICT

- Continue the whole-class session by brainstorming a list of images and ideas that are suggested by *Take Two*. Which are the most powerful images? Prepare to present the ideas to the rest of the class.

- Discuss reasons for the title of the poem. Why *Take Two*? (This could just describe the mixture of wind and rain, it could suggest a second try or having another go at something, this could be the second night of poor weather, etc.)

- As a group, decide at least three ways in which poetry is different from stories or other writing. Make a poster that illustrates this and include some examples.◆◆◆

Reading books

REFLECTING: *plenary*

- Share and discuss ideas about the most powerful images in *Take Two*. Does everyone agree?

- Refine the ideas about what makes poetry different from stories or other texts.

ASSESSMENT
- Explore the difference between the language of poetry and prose.
- Respond appropriately to poetry, both orally and in writing.

Classic and modern poetry

2/3

Focus
Text level
Poetry: classic poetry
T2, T6

Learning objectives
- to recognise the distinctive features of traditional poetry
- to examine some of these features in selected poems

TEACHING: *whole-class introduction*

Resources

- Ask the children to suggest any words which their parents or grandparents use which seem out of date to them. If necessary, provide some possible examples: *wireless, pop group, jolly*. Share these, and talk about how language changes over time.

- Discuss what the children understand by the term 'classic poetry'. Encourage responses about traditional language, perhaps historical settings, poems that are seen as 'great' or 'good', etc.

- Explain that classic poetry does not need to be 'difficult' – use *Ring a ring o'roses* as an example of a simple traditional poem. Ask them what clues there are that suggest it is old (use of *o'* as an abbreviation for *of*, reference to *posies*, the subject is the symptoms of the Great Plague).

- Read the first part of *The Listeners*. Ask the children to suggest anything that makes them realise the poem is old (e.g. language – '*champed*', '*smote*'; a traveller on horseback; a building with a turret).

    Big Book page 24

- Introduce *The Jabberwocky* from the Anthology. Explain that this is another example of a famous 'classic' poem, but it is completely different to *The Listeners*. It is a traditional story of a brave warrior killing a terrible beast, but Lewis Carroll uses 'nonsense' language to tell the story.

    Anthology pages 37-38

Classic and modern poetry

DEVELOPING: *group activities*

Resources

Note: both The Listeners *and* The Jabberwocky *could be used for extended work over several sessions. The activities below are intended as brief introductions to the poems.*

- Read *The Listeners* in the Anthology and discuss what happens in the poem – what is the traveller doing and what happens in the end? Write a collaborative summary of the poem to present to the rest of the class. (The group will probably need support at various points during this activity.) ◆

  Anthology pages 39-41

- Prepare a dramatic reading of *The Jabberwocky* for the rest of the class. Look carefully at the poem and try to work out what is going on, then allocate parts to each member of the group and rehearse the performance. ◆◆

  Anthology pages 37-38

- Collect words and phrases from traditional poems and put together a word bank of examples which can be displayed on the wall, or perhaps on a computer database. ◆◆◆

  Poetry anthologies

  ICT

REFLECTING: *plenary*

- Present the summary of the story in *The Listeners*. Does everyone agree with this version of the story? Does anything need to be added?

- Share and discuss the dramatic reading of *The Jabberwocky*. What else could be added to the reading to improve it?

ASSESSMENT
- Recognise some of the main features of traditional poetry.
- Closely examine some of these features through reading, presentation and examining language.

Classic and modern poetry

3/3

Focus
Text level
Poetry: patterns in poetry
T2/T7, 11

Learning objectives
- to identify different patterns of rhyme and verse in poetry
- to write poems based on the structure and style of poems read

TEACHING: *whole-class introduction*

Resources

- Remind the children of the classic and modern poetry they have examined in the previous two sessions: *Take Two, The Jabberwocky* and *The Listeners*. Explain that this session is about looking at patterns in poetry, then writing poems of their own.

- **Shared text:** read the first limerick by Michael Palin, about Justice Percival. Remind the children of what they already know about limericks: the familiar rhythm, the rhyme of lines 1 and 2 with line 5, and of lines 3 and 4 (AABBA). Read (or preferably write on the board) the second limerick about Bruce the poacher, and use it to highlight the rhyming pattern and stress that limericks are often humorous.

Anthology page 42

- Discuss other types of rhyming pattern. Use class poetry anthologies to share examples of rhyming couplets, choruses, alternate rhyme lines, and other patterns that the children can identify.

Poetry anthologies

- Shared writing: ask the children to think of a subject for a short poem you are going to write together (e.g. a limerick). Then think of a word to do with that subject and brainstorm in one minute as many words as possible that rhyme with it.

- Together, write the limerick, using those discussed as a model. Follow the pattern of rhythm and rhyme, and make sure it is humorous!

Classic and modern poetry

DEVELOPING: *group activities*

- Choose a favourite poem (perhaps one of the examples discussed in the whole-class session), write part of it and illustrate it.◆

- Write a simple rhyming poem, using ideas and words brainstormed in the whole-class session.◆

- Write a nonsense verse modelled on *The Jabberwocky*, using nonsense words and rhyme.◆◆

- Fill in the gaps in a limerick to complete the rhyming pattern, then write a new limerick using the framework provided.◆◆

- Investigate how many different rhyme schemes can be found and prepare a chart showing them, with examples.◆◆◆

Resources

Practice PCM 67

Practice PCM 68

Practice PCM 69

Poetry anthologies
ICT

REFLECTING: *plenary*

- Share some of the poetry written during the group session. Are the rhyming patterns followed appropriately? Could the poems be improved in any way?

- Discuss the results of the investigation into rhyme schemes.

Homework

- Write a rhyming poem based on *The End* by A.A.Milne.◆◆

Homework PCM 32

ASSESSMENT
- Examine different techniques and patterns in poetry, with a focus on rhyme.
- Apply some of these to their own poetry writing.

Poetry: range of forms

1/4

Focus

Text level
Poetry: strong patterns
T3/T4, 5, 6, 7, 14

Learning objectives

- to develop knowledge of different forms of poetry
- to explore poems with strong, regular patterns

TEACHING: *whole-class introduction*

Resources

Resources: collections of traditional verse and poetry anthologies containing a wide range of different forms.

- **Shared text:** introduce the theme of the unit by reading aloud and showing two or three poems that differ markedly in terms of form, choosing your own examples or some from the Big Book. Ask the children what differences they notice, encouraging them to focus not on content but on aspects of form, e.g. length, patterns of sound and language. Explain that poetry takes many different forms, and that they will explore some of them in this unit.

  Big Book
  page 25-27

- Use the Big Book page to introduce the first form: poems with strong, regular patterns. The two examples illustrate a rhyme and a song with a chorus. For each, ask what kind of a poem is this? What is it for? Why is it good for this purpose? What do you notice about the way it is written? Prompt the children to examine the pattern of rhythm, rhyme, repetition of word patterns. Read the poems together several times, trying to get the patterns and rhythm just right, and clapping out the beat.

  Big Book
  page 25

- Shared writing: together, invent and write a new verse for *Praise, Song of the Wind*, a traditional poem from Siberia, giving it a local relevance. Use the terms *verse, chorus, rhyme* and *rhythm* and ensure they are understood.

Poetry: range of forms

DEVELOPING: *group activities*

Resources

- Continue the whole-class shared writing activity by writing new verses for *Praise, Song of the Wind*, or write a new poem based on this model.◆

- Complete and extend a simple poem with a strong repeating pattern.◆◆

Practice
PCM 70

- Find other examples of poems with strong rhythm and repetition in the class collection. Choose a favourite and prepare a reading aloud. Examine how it is written, and be ready to present this information.◆◆

Poetry
anthologies

- Read a poem with a strong, regular pattern. Examine aspects of its form and write new verses.◆◆

Textbook
page 53

- Write new verses modelled on those in the poems in the Big Book and/or similar poems.◆◆◆

Big Book
page 25

REFLECTING: *plenary*

Poetry
anthologies

- Read aloud the poems found in anthologies; explain their patterns of sound and language. Discuss any new or unfamiliar features of the poems.

- Present and read aloud the new verses they have written themselves.

Homework

- Write an acrostics poem.◆◆

Homework
PCM 33

ASSESSMENT
- Develop knowledge and understanding of a range of poetry forms.
- Recognise, use and respond to regular patterns of rhyme, rhythm and repetition.

Poetry: range of forms

2/4

Focus
Text level
Poetry: rhyme
T3/T6,14

Learning objectives
- to investigate rhyming patterns in poetry
- write poems modelled on those read

Resources

TEACHING: *whole-class introduction*

- Recap the work on patterns in poetry from the previous session, and explain that this session will focus specifically on rhyme, and different ways of arranging rhyming words in poetry.

- Reinforce the children's basic understanding of rhyming words, e.g. by offering a word and asking for others that rhyme with it. Brainstorm a range of ideas and build up lists.

- **Shared text:** show and read aloud the poems on the Big Book page. Ask the children to identify the rhyming words in each verse, and then the different patterns of rhyme. Highlight the text in different colours to show this. Use terminology: *verse, stanza* (a verse with a repeated pattern), *rhyming couplet, rhythm.*

  Big Book page 26

- Show the children how to use letters of the alphabet to show the pattern of rhyme, e.g. AA/BB for couplets, ABA for *Feeding the family*, ABAB for *Brian*. Can they think of any other examples?

- Discuss the effect of rhyme on how you read poetry. Emphasise that rhyme is a way of patterning language, that it makes ideas memorable and stronger. Discuss examples of other rhyming poems from previous sessions to reinforce the point.

Poetry: range of forms

DEVELOPING: *group activities*

- Fill rhyming gaps in a poem, then compile lists of rhyming words.

- Rhyme challenge: brainstorm a list of rhyming words and then write a simple rhyming poem together, using as many of the words as possible.

- Read poems with a simple rhyming pattern. Identify and record the pattern and use this as a model for writing similar poems.

- Find examples of rhyming poems in the class collection. Identify the rhyming patterns and prepare a reading or recording. Be ready to explain how the rhyme works, with close reference to the text.

- Examine a poem with a more complex pattern of rhymes. Record the pattern and prepare a reading aloud of the poem.

Resources

Practice
PCM 71

Textbook
page 54

Poetry
anthologies

Textbook
page 55

REFLECTING: *plenary*

- Read (or present recordings of) the rhyming poems they have found. Present and explain the pattern of rhyme. What new patterns have been found? How do they work?

- Read aloud poems they have completed or written themselves. Discuss how the rhyming pattern goes: has it been followed accurately?

ASSESSMENT
- Recognise a variety of rhyming patterns in poetry by referring closely to the text.
- Use these patterns as a stimulus for modelled poetry writing.

Poetry: range of forms

3/4

Focus
Text level
Poetry: haiku
T3/T7

Learning objectives
- to recognise a simple form of poetry and its uses
- to investigate and write haiku

TEACHING: *whole-class introduction*

Resources

- Introduce the session by explaining that they are going to look at haiku, a kind of very short poem that originated in Japan. Explain that what matters in haiku is not patterns of rhyme or rhythm but the number of syllables and the way they are arranged.

- Ask the children what they can recall from previous work they have done on haikus. Check that the children can count syllables, by working through some words, e.g. names: *Sam, An/war, An/ge/la*.

- **Shared text:** read the first two haiku in the Big Book. Ask the children what they notice about them. Draw out the ideas that haiku are: three lines long, and usually just one sentence; about just one thing or image; arranged so that the last line often makes a link between the first two lines or shifts the focus.

- Ask the children to work out the pattern of syllables in the first two haiku, and explain that the rule is: 5 syllables in the first line; 7 in the second; and 5 in the third. Use the third haiku to illustrate the point that sometimes poets (especially ones writing in English, not in Japanese) do not obey the rule exactly.

Big Book page 27

- Shared writing: together, try writing a haiku, for example about something seen through the window.

Poetry: range of forms

DEVELOPING: *group activities*

- Count the number of syllables in words, and in the lines of a haiku. Compile short lists of words with a given number of syllables.◆

- Cut out and sort nine lines to make three haiku. (Note: a number of different responses are possible here, providing the basic haiku structure is used in each response.)◆◆

- Read other haiku that do not strictly follow the pattern. Write a haiku about animals, focusing on close observation.◆◆

- Find haiku in class poetry collections. Copy out one or two favourites, then design and illustrate pictures for them; be ready to present and explain them.◆◆

- Decide as a group on a subject to write haiku about. Brainstorm words, images and ideas, then write the haiku. Try to make them as interesting, unusual or unexpected as possible!◆◆◆

Resources

Practice PCM 72

Practice PCM 73

Textbook page 56

Poetry anthologies

ICT

REFLECTING: *plenary*

- Share and work out any words that they found difficult to divide into syllables. Discuss compiling a class list of such words.

- Present haiku that they have found or written. Do they follow the rules exactly?

ASSESSMENT
- Investigate and respond to a range of haiku.
- Write examples of haiku effectively, modelled on those read.

Poetry: range of forms

4/4

Focus
Text level
Poetry: poetry forms
T3/T14,15

Learning objectives
- to write poems using a range of styles and structures
- to produce polished poetry through revision

TEACHING: *whole-class introduction*

Resources

Big Book pages 25-27

- **Shared text:** recap the range of poetry styles, structures and patterns that have been discussed in the previous sessions.

- By now the children will have written several poems (or at least verses of poems). Explain that the focus of this session is on developing and revising these.

- Decide before the session begins on three poems written by the children (one from each of the previous sessions) to discuss and revise together. Choose ones which have some strong points and some areas for development. Write them on the board, flip chart or OHT.

- Read through and discuss each of these poems. What do they like about the way it is written? Can they see ways in which it could be improved? Focus attention on aspects of form and language:
  - patterns of rhythm and rhyme
  - patterns of language
  - word choice: what words could be cut/added/changed for a stronger, more vivid word?
  - clarity and ordering of words in the line
  - overall organisation of the poem or verse.

- Shared writing: mark up the draft, inserting, deleting, etc. If the verse/poem is short, write out the revised draft, and discuss. Is it better? In what ways?

Poetry: range of forms

DEVELOPING: *group activities*

Note: the core activity for the groups should be revising and refining some of the poems and verses they produced in the earlier sessions, although some varied activities are suggested below. Include ICT opportunities for drafting, revising and presenting where possible, over several sessions.

- As a group, choose a poem drafted in an earlier session and collaborate on revising it, e.g. changing or deleting words, reorganising words and lines, etc. Present the original draft and the finished version side-by-side for comparison.◆

- Fill gaps in a poem, considering word choice and rhyme pattern. Compare different solutions.◆◆

- Produced a finished polished version of an earlier draft of a poem, with particular attention on using powerful and figurative language.◆◆◆

Resources

Practice
PCM 74

REFLECTING: *plenary*

- Share poems they have revised, explaining changes they made and why.

- Discuss possibilities for organising a display of poetry drafts and finished versions.

Homework

- Read and examine a poem about machines. Choose a machine and write a short poem about it.◆◆

Homework
PCM 34

ASSESSMENT
- Experiment with different styles, structures and patterns when writing poems.
- Develop the process of revising and refining drafts of work to produced polished versions.

Newspapers

Focus
Text level
Non-fiction: newspaper texts
T1/T16, 17, 20

Learning objectives
- to identify and read different kinds of texts found in newspapers
- to identify a range of non-fiction text features

TEACHING: *whole-class introduction*

Resources

Resources: a variety of newspapers, national and local.

- Brainstorm a list of the different kinds of writing to be found in newspapers, e.g. news stories, sports reports, editorials, letters to the editor, feature articles, cartoons, review, television and other entertainment listings. Introduce and explain the correct terminology.

- **Shared text:** use a current local or national newspaper to illustrate some of these text types (some pages could be used as enlarged photocopies). Focus on some interesting examples.

  Newspapers

- Discuss some of the characteristic features:
  – *How can you tell what it is?*
  – *What is its purpose?*
  – *How is it written?* (This aspect is developed in following sessions of this unit.)
  Make links with other work on different kinds of information writing.

- Choose one of the articles for a brief, detailed discussion. Examine the headline, subheadings, how the story is introduced, lists, bullet points, captions, pictures and layout. Show how the aim of an article is to give lots of information and hold the reader's attention, so it must be set out as clearly as possible. (These points will be developed in the following sessions.)

Newspapers

DEVELOPING: *group activities*

Resources

- Using a copy of your local newspaper, answer a range of basic questions on text types.◆

- Look at a current local or national newspaper and make notes on the range of text types it contains.◆

- Find examples in a local or national newspaper of all or several of the different kinds of texts identified in the whole-class session. Cut them out, label and display them.◆◆

Newspapers

- Find an example of one of the chosen text types. Examine it in detail, and write a caption explaining its content, style and purpose. Cut it out and add it to the display created by the other group (above).◆◆

- Find a newspaper article containing as many of these features as possible: headline, lists, bullet points, captions, pictures. Use the article as the basis for a display, with captions explaining each text feature and its purpose.◆◆◆

Newspapers

REFLECTING: *plenary*

- Share the newspaper texts they have found; discuss their purposes, styles and content.

- Identify and discuss similarities and differences between the various newspapers they have been looking at. What kinds of texts do they all have? What kinds did they find in only one or a few?

ASSESSMENT
- Explore a range of newspaper text types.
- Identify and examine the key features of the texts.

Newspapers

2/4

Focus
Text level
Non-fiction: fact and opinion
T1/T19

Learning objectives
- to understand and use the terms *fact* and *opinion*
- to distinguish between fact and opinion in newspaper texts

TEACHING: *whole-class introduction*

Resources

- Write up two sentences that state a fact and express an opinion about the same subject, for example:
  - *Chelsea won the FA Cup in 1997.*
  - *I think Chelsea is the best football team in the world.*

  Ask what is different about these sentences. Guide the children to the understanding that the first states a *fact* (it is either right or wrong; its truth can be checked; no one could disagree with it); whereas the second expresses an *opinion* (people could have a different point of view; the truth of it cannot be checked).

- Shared writing: together, write similar contrasting fact and opinion sentences about other subjects e.g. other sports, hobbies, issues linked to other subjects.

- **Shared text:** use the Big Book page to develop these points in relation to a longer text. Introduce this as an example of a newspaper editorial. Prompt the children to identify sentences that state facts and sentences that express opinions. These could be highlighted in different colours. Are there any sentences where it is difficult to tell whether it is fact or opinion?

  Big Book page 28

- Ask the children to identify other examples of fact and opinion from their reading of newspapers in the previous session and more widely. Encourage correct use of the terms *fact* and *opinion*.

  Newspapers

Newspapers

DEVELOPING: *group activities*

Resources

- Using one of the newspapers studied in the previous session, find an article that consists mostly of facts, or one that consists mostly of opinions. Prepare to present it to the rest of the class.◆

  Newspapers

- Read a newspaper review of a pantomime and identify facts and opinions. Write a review, including both facts and opinions.◆◆

  Textbook page 57

- Re-read the editorial about road safety in the Big Book. Write a letter to the editor, expressing your own opinion.◆◆

  Big Book page 28

- Identify from the newspaper extracts collected in the previous session, a piece that includes both facts and opinions. Be ready to explain what the piece is about and how facts and opinions are used.◆◆

  Newspapers

- Highlight and list facts and opinions in another newspaper editorial, review or letter.◆◆◆

  ICT

REFLECTING: *plenary*

- Share newspaper extracts, discussing whether they contain facts or opinions or a mixture of both.

- Discuss how other media can include both facts and opinions, e.g. radio, television, film. What examples can the children suggest?

Homework

- Read a letter in a newspaper and write a reply to it.◆◆

  Homework PCM 35

ASSESSMENT
- Investigate newspaper texts and identify facts and opinions.
- Use the terms *fact* and *opinion* accurately.

Newspapers

3/4

Focus
Text level
Non-fiction: headlines and openings
T1/18, 21

Learning objectives
- to investigate newspaper headlines and opening sentences
- to examine purpose and language features of these

TEACHING: *whole-class introduction*

Resources

- **Shared text:** show the Big Book page with headlines and opening sentences from three newspaper stories.♦♦

- Focus on the headlines. What do the children think the story is going to be about in each case? Discuss how the headlines are written:
  - places where words (especially *the* and *a*) have been left out (how would you usually say it?)
  - very short words (*hurt, slams*) used where longer ones would be more usual (e.g. *injured, attacked*)
  - use of present tense (*slams*) where the past would usually be used.

  Ask the children to think why headlines are written in this style. Stress the idea that they need to be short (and often dramatic) to capture attention.

  Big Book page 29

- Next, focus on the opening sentences. Ask the children what they notice about the information they contain and the way they are written (opening sentences are usually long and packed with information) and the reasons for this (to hold the reader's attention and convey the main points of the story). Prompt them to identify and list all the different bits of information provided in each sentence.

- Shared writing: together, write headlines and opening sentences for news stories about recent events in the school or local neighbourhood.

Newspapers

DEVELOPING: *group activities*

Resources

- Search newspapers for interesting headlines. Examine how they are written; be ready to share ideas. Predict what the story is going to be about.◆

  Newspapers

- Search newspapers for interesting opening sentences. Examine how they are written; be ready to share ideas. Predict the rest of the story.◆

  Newspapers

- Examine and write notes on newspaper headlines. Write the headlines for some fictional stories of their choice.◆◆

- Examine and write notes on opening sentences; write opening sentences to go with the headlines they wrote in the whole-class session.◆◆

  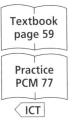

- Revise and shorten headlines and opening sentences.◆◆◆

REFLECTING: *plenary*

- Examine headlines and opening sentences found in newspapers. Discuss features of how they are written.

- Share the headlines and opening sentences they have written. How could they be improved?

Homework

- Write the opening paragraph of a newspaper report about a pollution scare at school. (This leads in to the next session on writing reports.)◆◆

ASSESSMENT
- Identify and discuss the characteristic features of newspaper headlines and opening sentences.
- Write headlines and opening sentences using these features.

Newspapers

4/4

Focus
Text level
Non-fiction: writing reports
T1/T24

Learning objectives
- to plan and write a newspaper report
- to use text features explored in previous sessions

TEACHING: *whole-class introduction*

Resources

- **Shared text:** use one or more of the newspaper texts from the previous sessions to recap on the main text features, including the headline, subheadings, how the story is introduced, lists, bullet points, captions, pictures, layout.

Newspapers

- Explain that news reports usually have a distinctive structure that makes them different from fictional stories. Instead of describing events in the order they happened (as in a story), news reports usually begin with a summary and then give information in order of importance, starting with the most important.

- Show how a plan for a news story can be made using the photocopiable sheets enlarged to A3:
  - a triangle, putting the most important information at the top and spreading out to give the least important information at the bottom
  - the five *Ws*: *What, When, Where, Who* and *Why*. A good news report should include information about all of these subjects.

Practice
PCM 78-79

Stress that newspaper reports should always be organised into paragraphs and that they are usually written to fill a certain space, e.g. of 100 words.

- Introduce and set up the group activities in which the children will plan and write a newspaper report about a recent event in the school or local neighbourhood. Brainstorm possible subjects.

Newspapers

DEVELOPING: *group activities*

Resources

Note: the two photocopiable sheets are designed to support children at the planning stage, depending on their ability level. The whole process of planning, writing and presentation is likely to take two or three sessions. Use ICT where possible.

- Plan a news report using the triangle frame to arrange information in descending order of importance. Write and present the news report.◆

  Practice PCM 78

- Plan a news report under headings for the five *Ws*: *What, When, Where, Who* and *Why*. Write and present the news report.◆◆

  Practice PCM 79

- Plan a news report using some or all of the techniques discussed in the whole-class session. If possible, use word-processing or page layout software to produce draft and final versions of the story.◆◆◆

REFLECTING: *plenary*

- Read the news reports; invite comments related to the issues discussed in previous sessions. Do they catch and hold the reader's interest? Do they follow the usual style of newspaper reports?

- Discuss ways of collecting the reports to make a class newspaper.

Homework

- Write a report about their favourite sport.◆◆

ASSESSMENT
- Plan, write and present a newspaper report.
- Use a wide range of techniques and styles when planning and writing.

Instructions

1/2

Focus

Text level
Non-fiction: reading instructions
T1/T22

Learning objectives

- to develop understanding of features of instructional texts
- to demonstrate these features by examining specific texts

TEACHING: *whole-class introduction*

Resources

Resources: a collection of books and leaflets including instructions, e.g. for scientific experiments, setting up equipment, etc.

- **Shared text:** read the instructional text in the Anthology (about taking fingerprints). Ask the children what this is for. How can they tell?

- To extend work on instructions from Stage 3, prompt the children to look in more detail at the stylistic and organisational features of the text, and to consider how they are suitable for its purpose. Discuss:
  - the introductory paragraph, which identifies the intended outcome of the experiment, and provides some background information
  - the listing of equipment and materials
  - sentences giving reasons for following the instructions
  - sentences explaining what happens, in sequence
  - sentences giving tips, including the safety warning and the time indication
  - sentences giving commands, e.g. '*Toast a ...*'
  - how information is presented differently in the list of equipment and the instructions themselves (e.g. '*white plastic bag*' in list; just '*bag*' in instructions).

Anthology
pages 43-44

- In each case, prompt children to consider why it is helpful to give this information at this point and what might happen otherwise.

Instructions

DEVELOPING: *group activities*

Resources

- Find examples of instructional texts. Write a note explaining how they are written and what devices the author has used to help the person following the instructions. Do they seem to be clear and helpful?◆

    Instructional texts

- Instruction search: find as many examples as possible of instructions in the classroom and around the school, e.g. on posters, notices. Write a list.◆

- Re-read the instructions for taking fingerprints and discuss how they could be improved to make them clearer. Prepare to present ideas to the class.◆◆

    Anthology pages 43-44

- Read an instructional text about making pure water. Write about the strategies used by the author and discuss the effectiveness of the instructions.◆◆

    Textbook page 60

- Make a collection of instructional texts. Write labels for them and find ways of classifying them.◆◆◆

REFLECTING: *plenary*

- Present and discuss their notes about instructional texts. What are the crucial features? Have they found different ways of achieving the same purpose (e.g. numbered or bulleted lists of steps)?

- Share and discuss examples of instructions around the school.

Homework

- Follow the instructions to draw a bedroom rug.◆◆

    Homework PCM 38

ASSESSMENT
- Recognise the key features of instructional texts.
- Explore and evaluate the features of a range of instructional texts.

Instructions

Focus
Text level
Non-fiction: writing instructions
T1/T25, 26

Learning objectives
- to write clear instructions
- to improve written instructions using styles and devices learned from reading

TEACHING: *whole-class introduction*

Resources

Anthology pages 43-44

- **Shared text:** refer back where appropriate to the instructional text in the Anthology. Encourage the children to bear in mind the needs of the reader/user of the instructions; to consider the pros and cons of alternatives; and the importance of clarity and completeness.

- Choose a topic for instructions based on recent curriculum activities, e.g. art techniques; making something in Design and Technology.

- Talk it through with the children, encouraging them to identify and consider what someone needs to know for the activity in question, e.g. important details, the order in which things need to be done, material or ingredients required.

- Shared writing: together, work through the process of planning and writing instructions for the chosen activity. Prompt the children to draw on what they have learned from reading instructions in the previous session:
  - how and where to start, e.g. with an introduction
  - what devices to use, e.g. numbered steps, pictures
  - the appropriate style, e.g. imperative verbs
  - tips and warnings for the reader/user.

- When a draft has been completed, read it through with the children and prompt them to identify any problems and ways of putting them right.

Instructions

DEVELOPING: *group activities*

Resources

Note: these activities provide opportunities for planning and beginning writing instructions. The writing activities themselves should be extended outside the literacy hour. Use opportunities for ICT where possible.

- Plan, write and revise instructions for an activity of their own choice. Refer to instructions examined in the previous session for ideas.◆

- Rewrite a report of an activity (making paper) as instructions, considering necessary shifts in style and format.◆◆

  Textbook page 61

- Choose *either* (a) an activity to write instructions about *or* (b) a set of instructions that are regarded as poor and need to be improved. Use the prompt sheet for help where necessary.◆◆◆

  Practice PCM 80

REFLECTING: *plenary*

- Share their experiences of writing instructions: which devices and styles did they use? Which did they find especially useful? What problems did they have? What solutions did they try?

- Present and read their instructions, inviting comments and suggestions for improvement.

Homework

- Read the text about Jawad's hobby and write some simple instructions about a hobby.◆◆

  Homework PCM 39

ASSESSMENT
- Write clear instructions.
- Use styles and strategies of instructions read to improve writing of their own instructions.

Using ICT

1/2

Focus
Text level
Non-fiction: reading
with ICT
T1/T23

Learning objectives
- to explore strategies required for reading on screen
- to employ some of these strategies and evaluate their effectiveness

Resources

TEACHING: *whole-class introduction*

- Discuss with the children what they understand about 'reading with ICT'. Many of them will suggest 'reading from a computer screen', but stress to them that the skills involved can be used in many other areas, e.g. electronic devices at home (e.g. programming video recorders from on-screen instructions); various computer information systems (e.g. screens at railway stations and airports, cashpoint machines, etc). What other examples can the children suggest?

- **Shared text:** discuss using a CD-ROM encyclopaedia, which most of the children should have experience of. Talk about the different ways they read from the screen, and how this compares to reading information from a printed page:
  - *scrolling:* because the screen is just a 'window' on the text, the mouse or arrow keys have to be used to 'scroll' up and down to find information
  - *mix of information:* some screens contain a great deal of information packed closely together, giving the reader the option of which to choose
  - *hyperlinks:* these are underlined references to another piece of text (e.g. additional information), that you can click on to be given that text
  - *sound and video:* these are sometimes included to add information to the text supplied
  - *changeable:* some texts can be changed on-screen, or copied and pasted into a word-processor to be adapted.

CD-ROM
encyclopaedia

Using ICT

DEVELOPING: *group activities*

Note: all these activities require use of the class ICT resources. They are intended as basic introductions that should be extended in other work where possible. Where resources are limited, these activities may need to extend outside the literacy hour. The checklist could be used or adapted to evaluate the CD-ROM used.

- Use the encyclopaedia to experiment with reading by scrolling up and down the screen to locate information. (A simple comprehension activity could be pre-set to test their skills in doing this.) ◆

- Find a section of the encyclopaedia that includes lots of information and choices on the same screen, e.g. contents list, summaries, hyperlinks to other areas of the disk. Discuss and make notes about strategies for reading such a screen, e.g. using conventions from reading books – locating contents list first, working logically and sticking to the focus of the search. ◆◆

- Explore and discuss 'multimedia' features of on-screen texts, e.g. sound and animation. Discuss how they help with reading the text and compile a list of advantages (e.g. hearing a musical instrument) and disadvantages (e.g. unnecessary video clips). ◆◆◆

Resources

Practice
PCM 81

CD-ROM
encyclopaedia

REFLECTING: *plenary*

- Discuss ideas about reading on-screen and how it is different to reading from books.

- Compile a class list of points and suggestions.

-ASSESSMENT
- Investigate strategies for reading on-screen.
- Use some of these strategies and evaluate their effectiveness.

Using ICT

2/2

Focus
Text level
Non-fiction: writing
with ICT
T1/T27

Learning objectives
- to write a non-chronological report using organisational devices
- to use ICT in writing and presenting the report

TEACHING: *whole-class introduction*

Resources

- Introduce the idea of a *non-chronological report*: a report or piece of writing that is organised by themes or topic, not time. For example, this might be a report about a town with headings about size, number of people, types of shops. (A chronological report is one with a time sequence, e.g. a football match report.)

- **Shared text:** use the shared non-fiction text to demonstrate these basic features of a non-chronological report.

    Shared text

- Brainstorm ideas for a non-chronological report that could be written during the group activities session, e.g. school fair report, a report on a local issue, book report, etc.

- Discuss ideas for using ICT to draft, design and present the reports. Ideas could include typing in the draft report and proofreading it before using formatting, different type styles and sizes, etc.; different styles of heading and subheading to attract attention and split up the information logically; using bulleted or numbered lists to organise and present details, etc.

- Introduce the idea of the children editing their own work, e.g. using a spellchecker, making general points about some details, deleting less important points, changing the order of points to give better emphasis, cutting text to fit the space available, etc.

Using ICT

DEVELOPING: *group activities*

Resources

Practice
PCM 82

Note: all these activities require use of the class ICT resources. They are intended as basic introductions that should be extended in other work where possible. Where resources are limited, these activities may need to extend outside the literacy hour. The checklist could be used or adapted to evaluate work.

- Use a simple word-processor to plan, draft and write a report about a favourite television programme. Use some of the features discussed with the whole class, e.g. different type styles and sizes.◆

- Explore the use of advanced word-processor functions, such as boxes, shading, use of pictures/symbols, to write a non-chronological report about a favourite book.◆◆

- Use page layout software to create a poster reporting on a recent school event, e.g. a summer fair or a Christmas play. Make sure the report is non-chronological and presents information as clearly as possible, e.g. using bulleted lists.◆◆◆

REFLECTING: *plenary*

- Share the different kinds of reports that have been written. How could they be improved?

- Discuss the different functions of the class word-processor and page layout software. How should the software be used sensibly (e.g. avoid using too many different type styles on a page)?

ASSESSMENT
- Recognise the characteristic features of a non-chronological report.
- Demonstrate this understanding, using ICT to draft and present a report.

Presentation of information

Focus
Text level
Non-fiction: instructions
T2/general

Learning objectives
- to investigate how information is presented
- to evaluate different examples of presenting instructions

TEACHING: *whole-class introduction*

Resources

- Begin the session by brainstorming all the different kinds of non-fiction information the children might come across in their work, e.g. instructions, letters, dictionaries, thesauruses, reports, recounts, information books, explanations, persuasion, discussion. Explain that this unit of work will focus on how information is presented in some of these text types (*instructions, explanations, recounts*).

- **Shared text:** read the page from the Big Book about rules for the treasure hunter. Discuss what a treasure hunter is and explore any unfamiliar vocabulary (e.g. *archaeological*). Ask the children to suggest anything they know about finding treasure.

- Look closely at the Big Book page. Discuss what type of non-fiction text this is (instructions) and how the information has been presented, e.g. clear heading, numbers to clearly list the points, direct verbs (*do not*), a box at the bottom to highlight important information, use of colour, and so on. Refer to work the children may already have done on instructions (see page 178 onwards).

  Big Book page 30

- Discuss other examples of instructions in the classroom and around the school. What presentation features do they use? Could they be improved in any way? How?

Presentation of information

DEVELOPING: *group activities*

- Write a list of instructions for behaving in the classroom, using the Big Book text as a model. Think carefully about how to present the instructions, e.g. for everyone to see them, they will have to be clearly set out on a poster.◆

- How could the Big Book instructions be improved? Discuss some ideas and prepare to present them to the rest of the class.◆◆

- Follow on from the whole-class session by identifying and evaluating some examples of posters from around the school. Which instructions could be improved? How?◆◆

- Write a list of instructions for presenting instructions! For example, set points out clearly and use illustrations.◆◆

- Research examples of instructions in class non-fiction books. Find at least one good example and one bad example to share with the rest of the class.◆◆◆

Resources

Big Book page 30

Big Book page 30

Practice PCM 83

ICT

Information books

REFLECTING: *plenary*

- Share and discuss ideas for how the Big Book text could be improved.

- Present good and bad examples of instructions, and discuss the reasons for these evaluations. Do the rest of the children agree?

ASSESSMENT
- Recognise typical formats of instruction texts.
- Discuss and evaluate some different formats and layouts.

Presentation of information

Focus
Text level
Non-fiction: explanations
T2/T20, 24, 25

Learning objectives
- to recognise how explanatory texts are presented
- to recognise how to order and sequence text in explanations

TEACHING: *whole-class introduction*

Resources

Practice
FCM 85

- **Shared text:** read the explanation about the literacy hour from the photocopied sheet, or enlarge it to A3 to share with the class.

- Discuss the main features of explanatory texts and how they are similar to and different from instructions, e.g.:
  - *aim:* to explain a process or answer a question
  - *structure:* the points are organised in sequence, each with a clear focus
  - language features: usually in the present tense, use of connectives of time (*first ... then ... at the end*)
  - *presentation:* sometimes use diagrams or illustrations, subheadings, numbering.

- Discuss with the children their understanding of the term 'sequence', e.g. getting up, having breakfast, coming to school. Encourage them to distinguish between essential information – without which the sequence doesn't make sense – and less important information (e.g. in the 'getting up' sequence, the breakfast cereal may not be important).

- Emphasise that it is particularly important for a writer to get the sequence of events right and to signal the sequence very clearly to the reader, e.g. through use of vocabulary like *first, next, lastly*; by using devices like numbered points or a list; by the use of headings.

Presentation of information

DEVELOPING: *group activities*

Resources

- Write a sequenced explanation on a subject of choice, using a simple writing frame. ◆

- Use the photocopied sheet as a model for writing an explanation of how they get to school every day. Remember to use the features of an explanatory text, e.g. clear sequence, present tense.◆

- Read the mixed-up explanation about researching a history topic, then re-organise the points.◆◆

- Use the class collection of non-fiction books to find and evaluate an explanation. Use the details from the whole-class session, e.g. is the aim of the explanation clear? Is the sequence clear and well-organised? Are paragraphs used?◆◆

Non-fiction books

- Use the information from the whole-class discussion to write an explanation about how to write an explanation! Present it in poster form as an *aide-memoir* for the rest of the class.◆◆◆

REFLECTING: *plenary*

- Ask the children to apply the points of this session to other work. Ask them to identify when it would be useful to organise writing in this way (e.g. when explaining how to play a game).

- Share and discuss the examples of explanations found in class non-fiction books. Has the group found both good and bad examples?

ASSESSMENT
- Recognise the key features of explanatory texts.
- Use these features in writing and organising explanations.

Presentation of information

3/4

Focus
Text level
Non-fiction: recounts
T2/T17, 19

Learning objectives
- to examine the presentation and structure of a recount
- to organise and present recounted information clearly

TEACHING: *whole-class introduction*

Resources

- **Shared text:** read the Anthology text about the Spanish Armada. Remind the children of the activity in the previous session about researching a history topic, and explain that this session will continue with the topic of the Spanish Armada. Discuss and explain any unfamiliar vocabulary.

  Anthology pages 45-46

- Discuss what the children understand as a 'recount', and explore the main features:
  – a clear heading to explain the subject of the text
  – an introduction to set the scene
  – the information is clearly organised in paragraphs
  – the paragraphs are in *chronological order* (explain this term)
  – the final paragraph is the conclusion that 'rounds off' the recount.

- Recap the Anthology text and demonstrate how these points are shown, e.g. clear chronological order. In this case the conclusion both 'rounds off' the text and introduces a new point of interest: the treasure hunter.

  Anthology pages 45-46

- Introduce the idea that recounts are not necessarily to do with history and can also be fictional. For example, you could describe most stories as a recount, because they retell certain details about events in a certain order. Share and discuss examples.

Presentation of information

DEVELOPING: *group activities*

- Write a short recount to show what happened in school yesterday. Make sure the information is clearly organised and in chronological order.◆

- Re-read the recount about the Spanish Armada that was shared in the whole-class session. Write new sub-headings for the different sections of the account and then write a summary.◆◆

- An account of the sinking of the *Girona* has been mixed up. Arrange the points in sequence.◆◆

- Research and locate two examples of recounts: one fiction, one non-fiction. Prepare to present them to the rest of the class, to show their main features.◆◆◆

- Using the text in the Anthology, retell the story of the *Girona* in no more than ten sentences. The sentences should build up to a continuous piece of prose, so the children should pay particular attention to the way they introduce the sequence.◆◆◆

REFLECTING: *plenary*

- Share and discuss examples of fiction and non-fiction recounts. Do they show similar features? Are any of them unusual in any way?

- Recap the importance of chronological order to recounts, using examples from the group work to reinforce the point.

Resources

Textbook pages 63-64

Practice PCM 86

Recount texts

Anthology pages 45-46

ASSESSMENT
- Investigate and understand how recount texts are presented and structured.
- Apply this understanding to both fiction and non-fiction texts.

Presentation of information

4/4

Focus
Text level
Non-fiction: presenting information
T2/T24, 25

Learning objectives
- to consolidate knowledge of information presentation
- to write explanations of a process, using conventions discussed

TEACHING: *whole-class introduction*

Resources

- **Shared text:** briefly recap one or all of the text types discussed in the previous 'presentation' sessions, e.g.:
  - *instructions:* re-read the Big Book text about treasure hunting
  - *explanations:* re-read the photocopiable sheet about the literacy hour
  - *recounts:* re-read the Anthology text about the Spanish Armada.
  Use the texts to remind the children of the key presentation features of each text type and clear up any confusion. You could also refer to the children's written work or texts located in previous sessions.

  Big Book page 30

  Practice PCM 85

  Anthology pages 45-46

- Explain that this session will be about creating and presenting information using one of these text types. Brainstorm a list of possible subjects:
  - *instructions:* e.g. classroom rules, road safety
  - *explanations:* how to use a word-processor, how to program a video, how to ride a bike
  - *recounts:* last summer's holiday, what happened last weekend, yesterday morning in school.
  Encourage the children to think of challenging or unusual topics that they might not usually consider.

- Shared writing: briefly remind the children of the process of planning, drafting and writing. Discuss alternative methods of presentation, e.g. flow diagrams, storyboards, etc.

Presentation of information

DEVELOPING: *group activities*

Resources

Note: the group activities are designed to form extended writing tasks that should be extended outside the initial literacy hour. Encourage the children to reflect on discussions about text types from the previous sessions and use these for ideas where necessary. Use opportunities for ICT where possible.

- Explanation: present a more detailed explanation of the literacy hour, as discussed in the previous sessions. What information could be added to improve the explanation (e.g. examples of activities)? What information is unnecessary (e.g. the names of people in the class)?◆

  Practice PCM 85

- Instructions: examine a badly-presented set of instructions and improve them.◆◆

  Textbook page 65

- Recount: write an extended recount of an historical event, related to a current history topic. Research and use reference books where necessary.◆◆◆

  Reference books

REFLECTING: *plenary*

- Pause the group work at various stages to check progress of planning, drafting and writing, and to reinforce points about presentation.

- Discuss different ways of presenting and sharing the finished writing, e.g. a class book, a display, etc.

Homework

- Complete the chart from a television guide and write two paragraphs about television programmes.◆◆

  Homework PCM 40

ASSESSMENT
- Review and consolidate knowledge of presentation of information.
- Write extended texts and present them effectively.

Information books

1/3

Focus
Text level
Non-fiction: choosing
texts for research
T2/T15,16

Learning objectives
- to appraise a non-fiction book for its contents and usefulness
- to prepare for factual research

TEACHING: *whole-class introduction*

Resources

Resources: a collection of information books about an environmental subject, e.g. recycling, transport, etc.

- Introduce the unit by explaining that the children will be learning how to carry out a research project into an environmental topic: recycling. (Note that some points here are touched on in the unit on Presentation of information, pages 188-189).

- Explain and discuss the first steps in such a research project, in relation to the topic of recycling:
  1) *Deciding* exactly what the topic of your research will be, keeping it sharply focused (e.g. materials that can and cannot be recycled; how a particular material is recycled).
  2) *Reviewing* what you know already about it and what you want to find out. Work through an example with the children, e.g. by listing in two columns. As a result of this, identify a small number of questions which the research will be aimed at answering.
  3) *Choosing* books and other resources likely to provide the information they want.

- **Shared text:** work through some examples of choosing books, considering whether particular books in the collection seem suitable for an identified purpose. Stress the information to be gained from the title and contents list, and from scanning headings. Include an example in which only a particular part of the book is relevant to the research.

Information books

Information books

DEVELOPING: *group activities*

- Choose and scan a book from the class collection. Write a note explaining how it would be useful in researching recycling: what part would be useful? ◆

- Read a selection of brief notes on books about recycling. Identify those that would be relevant for different aspects of recycling. ◆◆

- Read a contents list from a book about waste and recycling. Identify parts that would be relevant for different aspects of recycling. ◆◆

- Write a list of points to describe what the group already knows about recycling, what they aim to find out, and the kinds of books they need to look for. ◆◆

- Identify different kinds of books in this area and their characteristic features. Explain what each kind of book would be especially useful for. ◆◆◆

Resources

Information book

Textbook page 66

Textbook page 67

ICT

Information books

REFLECTING: *plenary*

- Share ideas about the usefulness of particular books for particular purposes.

- Identify and discuss strategies for assessing the likely usefulness of a book, e.g. title, contents list, headings.

Homework

- Draw a picture and make notes about a female relative based on the example provided. (This leads in to the following session on note-making.) ◆

Homework PCM 41

ASSESSMENT
- Examine and assess the usefulness of a particular non-fiction text.
- Prepare for research by reflecting on what is known and examining the books available.

Information books

2/3

Focus
Text level
Non-fiction: making notes
T2/T17, 18, 21, 23

Learning objectives
- to demonstrate strategies for reading and note-making for research
- to develop note-making skills

TEACHING: *whole-class introduction*

Resources

- Following on from the last session, explain that when they have decided on a topic, identified what they want to find out and chosen suitable resources, the next step is to read and make notes on the relevant sections.

- **Shared text:** read through the text in the Anthology. Explain that they need to identify and record the information that is important for their purpose. Demonstrate the following strategies:

   Anthology page 47

  1) *Scanning* the text for essential information, using headings and paragraphs as a guide.
  2) *Listing* key words and phrases (or highlighting or underlining them if the text can be marked).
  3) *Summarising* the information in note form: what can they leave out? What do they need to write down in order to be able to recall the essential information? Prompt the children to look at how the text is organised in paragraphs and to identify the essential information in each. Explain that (in a good piece of writing) paragraphs provide a useful guide to the content. Stress that they do not need to write in sentences when briefly summarising information.
  4) *Representing* the information in a different form, e.g. a concept/mind map showing how ideas are related, a flow diagram, or a picture with labels. The description in the Anthology lends itself to representation as a flow diagram.

Information books

DEVELOPING: *group activities*

Resources

- Read and make simple notes on the information text in the Anthology using one of the strategies introduced in the whole-class session.◆

  Anthology page 47

- Read a set of extracts about getting rid of rubbish. Underline key words and summarise ideas.◆◆

  Practice PCM 87

- Represent information in an extract as a flow diagram.◆◆

  Textbook page 68

- Identify and record in note form the key ideas in each paragraph of a text.◆◆

  Textbook page 69

- Locate an information text (book or computer) about recycling or pollution. Identify a key section of the text, scan it for information, list key points and then summarise it (as text or as a diagram) for presentation to the rest of the class.◆◆◆

  Information text

REFLECTING: *plenary*

- Share ideas about the process of using the reading and note-making strategies, considering examples of each in turn.

- Share and discuss information located and summarised in the information text.

Homework

- Read the information about Brown and Polar bears, then write notes and complete a chart to compare them.◆◆

  Homework PCM 42

ASSESSMENT
- Use strategies for locating and identifying important information in a text.
- Make notes and summarise information.

197

Information books

3/3

Focus
Text level
Non-fiction: investigating a theme
T2/T17, 18, 19, 21, 22

Learning objectives
- to apply research skills to a project
- to reflect on and evaluate the research process

TEACHING: *whole-class introduction*

Resources

- Set up this session by explaining that the children will now be going on to use what they have learned about locating information and summarising it by carrying out research in a project of their own choice. Prompt groups to consider the range of environmental topics listed in the first session, and to choose one to focus on in their research.

- Emphasise the main ideas and strategies covered in the previous two sessions:
  - Planning and preparing (from session 1): *deciding* the topic for research; *reviewing* what they already know; *choosing* texts to use.
  - Strategies for reading and making notes (from session 2): *scanning* for information, *listing* key points, *summarising* in note form, *representing* as text or diagram.

- **Shared text:** recap some of the main issues from the previous two sessions about locating and summarising information.

  Anthology page 47

- Demonstrate and explain again any strategies that the children seem to be unsure of, using class texts as examples where necessary.

- Introduce and explain the two planning sheets and how to use them during the group activities.

  Practice PCM 88-89

Information books

DEVELOPING: *group activities*

Note: the core activity involves children in planning and carrying out a small-scale research project, choosing a specific topic within a broader subject. The resources below provide support for this. The children will need to extend their work outside the literacy hour to complete their project. When they have finished the research, they should use information-writing skills developed in other units to present what they have found out.

- Use this sheet to note the topic of the research, the questions that need to be answered and the resources to use.◆/◆◆

- Use this sheet to review existing knowledge and what needs to be investigated in more detail.◆/◆◆

- Using strategies discussed in the whole-class session, discuss and decide the topic for research, review existing knowledge and choose some texts (including ICT sources where possible, e.g. Internet searches). Begin the research process.◆◆◆

Resources

Practice PCM 88

Practice PCM 89

ICT

REFLECTING: *plenary*

- Pause at various points in the research for children to share both what they are finding out in the course of their research and the strategies they are using to gain this information. What works well? What are the problems? How could they be overcome?

- When they have completed the research, ask them to review and evaluate the whole process.

ASSESSMENT
- Develop research planning and note-making skills from previous sessions.
- Apply these skills in a piece of extended research.

Persuasive writing

Focus
Text level
Non-fiction: style and vocabulary
T3/T18

Learning objectives
- to explore how writers use style and vocabulary to convince their readers
- to recognise differences in methods of persuasion

TEACHING: *whole-class introduction*

Resources

- **Shared text:** read the advertisement in the Big Book. Ask the children to suggest what kind of text it is. What is it trying to persuade people to do?

- Discuss how the advertisement tries to persuade people to buy Soapy. For example:
  - *What* does it promise? (Soapy is new, cleans stains, better for the environment, you can get money off your next purchase.)
  - *How* does it give the information (bright colours, big headline to attract attention, 'flashes' and shapes containing information, bulleted list with repetition of name 'Soapy', illustration of product, use of logo).

Big Book page 31

- Do the children think this is a successful advert? Would it persuade them to buy Soapy?

- Together, list examples of words that are often used to persuade someone who is thinking of buying something. (Some examples to prompt them with could include: *money off, you cannot afford to miss!, sale, bargain, new,* etc.)

- An alternative approach to this part of the session would be to video-record some television advertisements and discuss them (instead of or as well as the Big Book page).

ICT

Persuasive writing

DEVELOPING: *group activities*

Resources

- With a partner, think about a game or a toy that they have grown out of. Think of ten words that would make it seem attractive to someone else. Make a 'For Sale' poster, including a picture of the toy and the words to describe it.◆

- With a partner, write a brief letter to the head teacher, trying to persuade him or her to change something in the school, e.g. improve playground facilities.◆◆

- Design a simple questionnaire to find out people's opinions about magazine or television advertisements.◆◆

- Find an advertisement that has recently been used around the school, e.g. for a school event. Evaluate it: is it successful or not? In what way? How could it be improved?◆◆

- Plan the content of a leaflet for children called *How to Persuade People in An Advert*. Focus on the use of style and vocabulary.◆◆◆

REFLECTING: *plenary*

- Discuss the advertisements investigated or created in groups. Recap the main features of style and vocabulary.

- Together, list all the things that make a good advertisement.

ASSESSMENT
- Recognise different ways by which writers persuade their readers.
- Investigate ways in which these methods are applied by advertisers.

Persuasive writing

2/3

Focus
Text level
Non-fiction: evaluating advertisements
T3/T19

Learning objectives
- to evaluate a range of advertisements
- to recognise the range of strategies advertisers use in selling products

TEACHING: *whole-class introduction*

Resources

Resources: a range of different advertisements from newspapers and magazines, plus (if possible) pre-recorded television and/or radio advertisements.

- **Shared text:** remind the children of the main features of an effective advertisement from the previous session.

    Big Book page 31

- Share a copy of the photocopied sheet (either distribute these to groups or use an enlarged A3 photocopy). Briefly talk through the sheet and explain that this is a checklist to be used when examining an advertisement.

    Practice PCM 90

- Together, look closely at one of your newspaper or magazine advertisements (or have the children watch or listen to a recorded advertisement). Establish what the advertisement is trying to sell and what its main features are, then work through the prompts on the photocopied sheet.

    Advertisements

- Repeat with another advertisement if you have time, preferably one with some different features.

- List with the children the ways in which advertisers try to persuade, e.g. making the viewer/reader/listener laugh through word play; jingles and music; invented words; alliteration (repetition of sounds at the beginning of words). Encourage the children to think of examples.

Persuasive writing

DEVELOPING: *group activities*

- Use the photocopiable sheet to evaluate an advertisement. (Differentiation will depend on the advertisement chosen.) ◆/◆◆

- In pairs, choose two or three magazine advertisements. Cut out some of the important words. Pass the advertisements to another pair and ask them to write some new persuasive text to fit. ◆

- Look carefully at two different advertisements. Answer questions about them and evaluate them using the sheet. ◆◆

- From the class collection of newspapers and magazines, find two examples of good advertisements, and two examples of bad ones. Write the reasons for them being good or bad, and prepare to present them to the rest of the class. ◆◆

- Find some examples of newspaper or magazine advertising that make exaggerated claims. ◆◆◆

Resources

Practice PCM 90

Magazines

Textbook page 70

Practice PCM 90

Newspapers
Magazines

Newspapers
Magazines

REFLECTING: *plenary*

- Share examples of good and bad advertisements.
- Discuss the criteria for good advertisements. (This leads into the activities in the next session.)

Homework

- Answer questions to evaluate an advertisement. ◆◆

Homework PCM 43

ASSESSMENT
- Evaluate a range of different advertisements critically.
- Identify and explore a range of different advertising techniques.

Persuasive writing

3/3

Focus
Text level
Non-fiction: writing
advertisements
T3/T25

Learning objectives
- to consolidate knowledge of persuasive writing techniques
- to apply these techniques in designing an advertisement

TEACHING: *whole-class introduction*

Resources

- **Shared text:** remind the children of the features of successful advertisements from the previous two sessions. Recap the kinds of style and language used and see how many details the children can recall and identify without prompting.

  Newspapers
  Magazines

- Give three children a different item each:
  – a can of cola
  – a chocolate bar
  – a good story book.
  Ask each of them to tell the rest of the class as many reasons as possible for drinking/eating/reading their item.

- Discuss how many different ways there are of persuading someone to buy something (television advertisement, radio, cinema, Internet, advertisement in a shop window, sandwich boards, sports sponsorship, etc).

- Explain that the rest of the session will be devoted to writing their own advertisements. The first decision will be what they are trying to sell: it might be a school event, or an imaginary new product, or a service of some kind. Explain that each group will have a role in the exercise. Remind them again of the criteria for effective advertisements.

Persuasive writing

DEVELOPING: *group activities*

Note: the whole class could collaborate on advertising a single product, or each group could concentrate on a different product. Some of the writing work might need to be extended outside the literacy hour. Use ICT where possible.

- Make a large poster to advertise the product or service, using the style, design and language features discussed in the previous sessions.◆

- Prepare a storyboard for a television advertisement (this could be video recorded with a camcorder, or performed for the class).◆/◆◆

- Write, rehearse and record on tape a one or two minute radio advertisement for the product or service.◆◆

- Design a magazine advert on the computer, using a range of type styles and sizes, illustrations, colour, etc.◆◆◆

REFLECTING: *plenary*

- Share the work produced by each group.

- Encourage the children to evaluate their work in the light of the advertisement analyses in the previous sessions.

Homework

- Design an advertisement for a favourite interest or hobby.◆◆

Resources

Practice
PCM 91

Homework
PCM 44

ASSESSMENT
- Use a variety of writing skills to persuade convincingly.
- Design, produce and evaluate a range of advertisements.

Discursive writing

1/4

Focus
Text level
Non-fiction: introducing discursive writing
T3/T16

Learning objectives
- to investigate discursive writing and some of its characteristics
- to recognise the difference between discussion text and argument text

TEACHING: *whole-class introduction*

Resources

- Introduce the children to the term *discursive writing* or *discussion text* – writing which discusses something and presents all sides of an issue. Link this to the children's understanding of an oral discussion. Ask what sorts of things could be discussed – highlight and reinforce answers that suggest that a discussion is a sharing, sometimes of news, opinions or ideas. Explain that *discursive writing* is similar: the sharing and balancing of ideas and opinions.

- Explain the difference between a text for discussion and a text for argument:
  - *Discussion* is about presenting all sides of an issue, points for and against.
  - *Argument* is about presenting one point of view and trying to persuade the reader.

- **Shared text:** use the shared text to illustrate these points. The two letters present very different arguments about the hunting of whales. Read them through, but before considering them in detail ask the children to suggest anything they know about whales or the hunting of them. Explain that whales are now so few in number because of hunting, that most hunting has been banned.

  Big Book page 32

- Read the Anthology page to illustrate a discussion text that balances both points of view. Discuss how this contrasts with the texts on the Big Book page.

  Anthology page 48

Discursive writing

DEVELOPING: *group activities*

- Write a simple letter to *World Wildlife News* that explains the two points of view about whaling.◆

- Hold a discussion about hunting and make notes about the main points. What do the members of the group already know about hunting? What do they need to find out? Make sure they are clear on the distinction between a *discussion* and an *argument*.◆◆

- Read the extract about the hunting of whales and then prepare a presentation about it for the rest of the class. Use other information books if necessary.◆◆

- Re-read the letters in the Big Book. Explain unfamiliar vocabulary, then identify where the writers are drawing on facts about whales, and where they are introducing their own ideas or opinions.◆◆

- Prepare a presentation for the rest of the class to explain what a discussion text is. Use examples from information books where possible.◆◆◆

REFLECTING: *plenary*

- Share and discuss ideas about what a discussion text is and what its main features are (presents all sides of an issue, gives arguments for and against, etc).

- Give a presentation about whaling, based on the Anthology text. Is the discussion fair and balanced?

Resources

Anthology page 48

Information books

Big Book page 32

Information books

ASSESSMENT
- Recognise how facts or information are selected to support an argument or point of view.
- Investigate and identify the principle features of discursive writing and how it differs from argument.

rsive writing

2/4

Focus
Text level
Non-fiction: presenting arguments
T3/T17

Learning objectives
- to investigate how arguments are presented
- to find and discuss examples of arguments

TEACHING: *whole-class introduction*

Resources

- **Shared text:** recap the Big Book text and ask the children to recall from the previous session that the two letters are arguments about different points of view on hunting whales.

- Look carefully at how each argument is presented on the Big Book page. Even though they are very brief, the letters are very clearly structured:

  Big Book page 32

  – *introduction:* a paragraph that introduces the writer's point of view about whaling
  – *main paragraph:* the first sentence gives the main point of the argument, then the next sentences add more detail
  – *final sentence:* this summarises the argument.

- Discuss what other devices the letter-writers could have used to support their arguments and try to persuade the reader. Use examples from class texts where possible and ask the children to contribute ideas from their own writing, e.g.:
  – introducing points clearly and using paragraphs to organise and build up ideas (as in the Big Book)
  – use numbered or bulleted lists to show points
  – use diagrams, pictures or photographs as evidence
  – use statistics, graphs, etc, to support arguments.

  Information books

- Ask the children to suggest arguments that they have read or taken part in, e.g. about a school issue.

208

Discursive writing

DEVELOPING: *group activities*

- How could the letters in the Big Book be improved? Discuss some ideas and prepare to present them. ◆

- Choose one of the letters from the Big Book page and write a reply to it, using the ideas about structuring arguments already discussed. ◆◆

- Use texts from the class or school library to investigate arguments about whales. Find examples with as many of the features discussed as possible, e.g. graphs, statistics, linked ordered points, bulleted or numbered lists, etc. ◆◆

- As above, but use newspapers and magazines to locate examples and identify features. ◆◆

- Prepare a presentation about using arguments to support a point of view and persuade other people. Include ideas and examples about the main features of arguments. Use a tape recorder to practise. ◆◆◆

Resources

Big Book page 32

Information books

Newspapers Magazines

ICT

REFLECTING: *plenary*

- Discuss ideas for how the letters in the Big Book could be improved, e.g. using diagrams or other evidence about the numbers of whales.

- Present the information about using arguments to support a point of view and persuade other people. Have all the main points been covered? Explain that these strategies will be used in later sessions in writing arguments of their own.

ASSESSMENT
- Explore strategies for presenting and organising arguments.
- Investigate a range of examples to illustrate the points.

Discursive writing

3/4

Focus

Text level
Non-fiction:
understanding arguments
T3/T20, 24

Learning objectives

- to understand arguments and identify the key points
- to summarise arguments clearly and concisely

TEACHING: *whole-class introduction*

Resources

- **Shared text:** recap some of the previous work about hunting whales. Recall some of the sources of information about whales that the children have used and the various pieces of discursive writing they have read. If the children have researched or debated the topic in subsequent work, recap details from these sources too.

  Shared text

- Explain that one of the key skills in reading and understanding arguments is being able to recognise the key points that the argument is making and summarising it. In this way, you can see clearly what the points are and make up your own mind.

- Collectively, brainstorm a list of points for and against the practice of hunting whales (or another topic), drawing on the children's experience of texts from the previous sessions. Write up the main points.

- Encourage the children to recognise that there are always likely to be different points of view about lots of issues. For example, although there is now a growing agreement about saving whales, people from different places might argue differently.

- Recap the points from the first session and point out that what the children are doing now is holding a *discussion* – talking about all sides of an issue, and examining the points for and against.

Discursive writing

DEVELOPING: *group activities*

- Continue the whole-class session by finalising the summary of the discussion about hunting whales. Present the summary on a poster and illustrate it.◆

- Re-read the Anthology text and write a list of points that summarise the arguments for and against.◆

  Anthology page 48

- Read a number of different views about hunting whales. Discuss and summarise the main arguments being used and then draw on existing knowledge to support or argue against these views. Prepare to present their argument to the rest of the class.◆◆

  Textbook pages 71-72

- Working in pairs, read the four arguments on the Textbook page, then write a note to explain the key idea of each argument. Explain which is the strongest argument, and why.◆◆

  Textbook page 71

- Use one of the information books from the previous session, and write a summary of one of the arguments it contains.◆◆◆

  Information books

REFLECTING: *plenary*

- Discuss different ways of summarising arguments: straightforward sentences, 'for' and 'against' charts, diagrams, etc.

- Share and discuss some of the summaries written.

Homework

- Examine contrasting ideas about school uniform.◆◆

  Homework PCM 45

ASSESSMENT
- Investigate and understand the key points of arguments.
- Write clear and effective summaries of arguments.

Discursive writing

4/4

Focus

Text level
Non-fiction: writing an argument
T3/T21, 22, 23

Learning objectives

- to assemble information and plan the presentation of a point of view
- to present a point of view in writing

TEACHING: *whole-class introduction*

Resources

- **Shared text:** use the Big Book page to recap the distinction between discussions and arguments from the first session of this unit.

  Big Book page 32

- Recap all the various pieces of work about hunting whales undertaken in previous sessions. Recall how in presenting an argument, writers draw on both factual information and their own ideas to make their points. Ask the children to recall some of the details they have learned about whales, and perhaps reinforce their growing awareness of how the same facts can be variously interpreted.

- Focus the children's attention on how a writer not only uses information, but also *interprets* it in order to present an argument. Recall the use of unsupported opinions and emotive comments (the Big Book letters), and the presentation of different points of view (the Anthology text). Ask the children to suggest other examples they have come across in their research, e.g. use of graphs and statistics in information books, headlines in newspapers.

  Big Book page 32

  Anthology page 48

- Explain that the group activities will involve the children researching and writing their own arguments. This will involve:
  - finding the information
  - gathering points and putting them in order
  - presenting the points, e.g. as a letter or report.

Discursive writing

DEVELOPING: *group activities*

Note: the focus of the group activities is on researching, gathering, organising and presenting points as an argument of a particular point of view. The planning/drafting phase should be followed up with writing the full report. This work will need to be extended across several sessions outside the initial literacy hour. Use opportunities for ICT where possible.

- Use a simple drafting frame to gather ideas and suggestions for a written argument about a chosen point of view. The topic could reflect recent work, (e.g. hunting whales) or be a personal choice.◆

  Practice PCM 92

- Use a writing frame to gather ideas for a written argument.◆◆

  Practice PCM 93

- Working in pairs, consider a particular theme or topic from a number of different points of view, drafting the main arguments.◆◆◆

  Practice PCM 94

REFLECTING: *plenary*

- Interrupt the planning and drafting stages at various points to discuss progress and identify areas of concern or confusion.

- Discuss ideas for presenting the written arguments, e.g. as a straightforward report, as a letter, as a newspaper article, etc.

Homework

- Answer questions about noise pollution.◆◆

  Homework PCM 46

ASSESSMENT
- Plan, draft and prepare points for a written argument.
- Produce an effective written argument that is clearly organised.

Teaching and learning literacy

The National Literacy Strategy

The NLS framework for teaching offers the following advice on the teaching and learning of literacy.

What is literacy?

Literacy unites the important skills of reading and writing. It also involves speaking and listening. Good oral work enhances pupils' understanding of language in both oral and written forms and of the way language can be used to communicate. It is also an important part of the process through which pupils read and compose texts.

Literacy requirements

Literate primary children should:
- read and write with confidence, fluency and understanding
- be able to orchestrate a full range of reading cues (phonic, graphic, syntactic, contextual) to monitor their reading and correct their own mistakes
- understand the sound and spelling system and use this to read and spell accurately
- have fluent and legible handwriting
- have an interest in words and their meanings, and a growing vocabulary
- know, understand and be able to write in a range of genres, and understand and be familiar with some of the ways in which narratives are structured through basic ideas of setting, character and plot
- understand, use and be able to write a range of non-fiction texts
- plan, draft, revise and edit their own writing
- have a suitable technical vocabulary through which to understand and discuss reading and writing
- be interested in books, read with enjoyment and evaluate and justify their preferences
- through reading and writing, develop their powers of imagination, inventiveness and critical awareness.

| **Teaching strategies** | Teachers will need to use a wide range of strategies to ensure high levels of motivation and active engagement of all pupils. These include:
- **direction:** e.g. to ensure pupils know what they should be doing, to draw attention to points, to develop key strategies in reading and writing
- **demonstration:** e.g. to teach letter formation and join letters, how to read punctuation using a shared text, how to use a dictionary
- **modelling:** e.g. discussing the features of written texts through shared reading of books, extracts
- **scaffolding:** e.g. providing writing frames for shared composition of non-fiction texts
- **explanation** to clarify and discuss: e.g. reasons in relation to the events in a story, the need for grammatical agreement when proofreading, the way different kinds of writing are used to serve different purposes
- **questioning:** to probe pupils' understanding, to cause them to reflect on and refine their work, and to extend their ideas
- **exploration:** initiating and guiding this, e.g. to develop phonological awareness in the early stages, to explore relationships between grammar, meaning and spelling with older pupils
- **investigating ideas:** e.g. to understand, expand on or generalise about themes and structures in fiction and non-fiction
- **discussing and arguing:** e.g. to put points of view, argue a case, justify a preference
- **listening to and responding:** e.g. to stimulate and extend pupils' contributions, to discuss/evaluate their presentations.

Adapted from The National Literacy Strategy: framework for teaching (DfEE 1998) |
|---|---|

The literacy hour

Structure of the hour

The literacy hour is designed to provide a practical structure for time and class management and should be implemented throughout the school to provide a daily period of dedicated literacy teaching time for all pupils, as advised in the NLS framework for teaching.

1. Shared text work

Whole class: about 15 minutes
Shared reading is a class activity using a common text, e.g. a big book, poetry poster or text extract. For younger pupils, teachers should read with the class and focus on comprehension and specific features of words, sentences and the whole text. For older pupils, shared reading is used to extend reading skills, and to teach and reinforce grammar, punctuation and vocabulary work.

Shared writing provides opportunities to learn, apply and reinforce skills with the whole class. Using texts for ideas and structures, pupils should compose texts with careful guidance from the teacher and with attention to planning, sequence and structure. Shared writing can also be used to reinforce grammar and spelling skills, demonstrate layout and presentation and stimulate independent writing. It should be linked to shared reading wherever possible.

2. Focused word or sentence work

Whole class: about 15 minutes
For younger children, this should involve a systematic, regular and frequent teaching of phonological awareness, phonics and spelling. For older children, this time should be used to cover spelling and vocabulary work, plus grammar and punctuation. Teachers should plan effectively to ensure a balance of word and sentence work across each half term.

3. Group and independent work	*Ability groups: about 20 minutes* *Independent work:* reading, writing or word and sentence work. Pupils should work independently and not interrupt the teacher. Organisation depends on the particular needs of each class, and could range from groups organised in a 'carousel' (with a rotation of activities around the groups each week), through to paired or completely independent work. *Guided work:* this should be in the form of guided reading or guided writing. *Guided reading* involves the teacher working closely with one ability group, with each pupil reading from individual copies of the same text. *Guided writing* should normally be linked to reading and should be used to meet specific learning objectives and focus on specific aspects of the writing process, rather than on the completion of a single piece of work.
4. Plenary session	*Whole class: about 10 minutes* This final part of the session should be used to spread ideas, re-emphasise teaching points, clarify misconceptions and develop new teaching points. It should enable pupils to reflect on what they have learned, revise and practise new skills, share work and provide constructive feedback and encouragement to their peers. **Note:** *the literacy hour is intended to be a time for the explicit teaching of reading and writing. Teachers will need to provide opportunities for practising and applying new skills at other times, including extended reading and writing linked to other curriculum areas.* *Adapted from The National Literacy Strategy: framework for teaching (DfEE 1998)*

Range of text types

Text type	Narrative	Recount	Instruction
Purpose	To entertain, possibly to teach/inform, to extend imagination.	To retell an event, or series of events.	To tell someone how to do or make something.
Structure and organisation of the text	• Focus: a sequence of actions • Orientation: setting the scene • Series of events containing a complication or problem • Resolution	• Focus: a sequence of events relating to a particular occasion • Orientation: giving background information • Series of events in chronological order	• Focus: a sequence of actions • Aim – indicated in main heading or title • Materials – listed in order of use • Method • Headings, sub-headings, numbers, diagrams, photos, etc, used to help understanding
Language features	• Narrative has specific characters • Mainly action verbs, e.g. *ran, strode, drove* • Verbs describing characters' speech and feelings, e.g. *asked, pleaded, demanded, wept, begged* • Normally past tense • Linking words related to time, e.g. *first, later that day, afterwards, etc* • Descriptive language, use of metaphor/simile • Can be written in first or third person	• A recount has specific characters • Mainly action verbs • Normally past tense • Linking words related to time • Precise details of time and place • Descriptive detail for precision and interest • Can be written in first or third person	• Reader referred to in a general way – one/you, sometimes not addressed at all, e.g. *glue paper* • Mainly action verbs, e.g. *put, place, glue, whisk, take* • Verbs often begin sentences • Simple present tense • Linking words to do with time • Detailed factual descriptions • Detailed information on how, where, when
Examples	Tend to be imaginary: fairy tales, myths, legends, science-fiction, short stories, adventure stories	Diary, journal, science experiment, biography, autobiography, historical account	Recipes, experiments, games rules, craft instructions, directions

Text type	Non-chrono-logical report	Explanation	Persuasive/discursive
Purpose	To document, organise and store information.	To give an account of how or why something works or happens.	To take a position on an issue and justify it.
Structure and organisation of the text	• Focus: a class of 'things' rather than a sequence • Opening general statement/general classification • Facts about various aspects of the subject grouped into topic areas • A general statement may round it off • Paragraphs, subheads, diagrams, photos, illustrations, etc, used	• Focus: main focus is on a process rather than an object • Opening statement about the item under discussion • Sequenced explanation, usually chronological	• Focus: taking an issue and forming a logical related argument • Statement of problem/issue • Statement of position • Argument(s) with evidence, reasons, statistics • Summary • Persuasive texts offer one point of view, discursive texts offer two or more views
Language features	• Generalised rather than specific participants, e.g. birds, castles, etc • Some action verbs, e.g. *fly, feed, live* • Some linking verbs, e.g. *is, has* • Usually in simple present tense • Descriptive language, but factual and precise • Language for defining, classifying, comparing and contrasting • Likely to contain technical vocabulary • Fairly formal style – first person pronouns and 'writer's voice' not appropriate	• Mainly action verbs • Usually simple present tense • Language relating to time • Cause and effect relationships, e.g. *due to ..., once the ... the, if*, etc	• Variety of verbs, e.g. action, linking, etc • Mainly simple present tense, but may change according to presentation of points • Language associated with reasoning, e.g. *therefore, so, due to* • Use of emotive vocabulary, e.g. *should, must, it is essential that ...* • Use of technical terms
Examples	'Topic' books, e.g. *Animals of the Desert*, *Plants we Eat*	*Why Volcanoes Happen*, *How Cows Make Milk*	Adverts, flyers, brochures, letters, etc, persuading the reader to do, think or take action

ICT and literacy

What is ICT?

ICT is **Information and Communications Technology.** The 'C' in ICT reflects both recent technical innovations such as e-mail, as well as a more considered view of how information technology relates to key skills such as literacy, and how the technology can best be harnessed and used productively.

Introduction

It is crucially important that we understand the contribution of ICT to the learning process and the role it will play as a key tool in the lives of our children in the new millennium. A consensus is emerging amongst educationalists and employers that the four key life skills are literacy, numeracy, communication and IT skills.

Password English identifies opportunities for using ICT in its broadest sense in many of the literacy hour sessions, including the use of tape recorders and other devices alongside the use of computers. It is important to note that these are by no means the *only* opportunities for integrating ICT into the literacy hour, but just a selection of key activities and opportunities. The activities are designed with the assumption that a classroom may have access to only one computer.

The information on the following pages is intended as a very brief introduction to the use of computers in literacy teaching and learning in primary schools. With a constantly evolving technology it is impossible to provide a comprehensive overview, but the key ICT skills can usefully be summarised as follows:
- exploration
- publication
- communication.

Exploration

One of the great potential benefits of ICT is the ability to explore and process huge amounts of information, relatively easily and quickly, e.g. using CD-ROM sources or the Internet.

One of the potential dangers, however, is that children will use the technology without being clear about its purpose and intended outcomes. The PC is a tool and should be used as such. For example, it may be the case that information can be better accessed by using traditional sources (such as the school library) rather than an electronic encyclopaedia.

If an electronic encyclopaedia or other information source is an appropriate resource, children must then know *how* to research and locate the required information. Printing verbatim from a CD-ROM is as futile as copying from a textbook. Information needs to be read, evaluated, sifted and processed in the same way as when using a traditional printed source.

With the increasing use of electronic information sources, including the Internet, it will be necessary to give our notion of 'reading' a wider definition. Text can be paper-based, but it can also be screen-based. The new definition of reading must acknowledge that reading from a screen also involves skills such as navigating (e.g. scrolling up and down to find information), handling non-linear texts (e.g. following hypertext links to other CD-ROM sections or Internet sites) and dealing with integral graphics, animations, sound and video.

ICT and literacy

Publication

The concept of 'publication' includes composing, transforming and presenting texts. This should not be limited to using a simple word-processor to produce a finished version of work for display. It could include, for example:

- **planning:** brainstorming and planning initial ideas, either individually or in groups
- **drafting:** producing an initial version that can later be edited and amended on-screen
- **writing:** this could range from children working individually and simply typing a story into a word-processor, through to sophisticated collaborative writing activities in which different children contribute to a piece of work (either on-site or via e-mail)
- **transforming:** this could include changing a narrative into a drama script, selecting factual points from a piece of fiction to turn it into a newspaper story, or editing and reworking texts for different audiences
- **presenting:** this could range from using basic word-processor functions (such as different text sizes, bold, italic, underline and colour) to produce posters or other information texts, through to using spreadsheets or databases to present information and research findings.

A number of basic computer skills are critical to underpinning such activities, including familiarity with using a mouse and basic keyboard skills. The better children become at using a keyboard, the more effective and rewarding their 'publication' work will become!

Commun-ication	Communication in its broadest sense includes all of the 'publication' issues mentioned on the preceding page. Children should understand this broad definition of using ICT for communication, as well as more precise definitions, such as using e-mail.

E-mail (or electronic mail) is a powerful and flexible aspect of the Internet that can be used for a wide range of purposes:
- **simple communication:** electronic messages can be sent cheaply and quickly to and from any computer in the world with an Internet connection
- **sharing information:** text files, pictures and even sound and video files can be electronically attached to an e-mail and sent anywhere in the world
- **collaboration:** using the above methods, children can now work together on projects, across geographical boundaries.

Other methods of communication include message boards and 'newsgroups' that can be used to research and request information. Simulations can be used, either in the classroom or across the Internet, to mirror real-life events and test the children's communication and collaboration skills. |
| **The Internet** | With the development of the National Grid for Learning, the Internet will become an essential classroom resource to encompass the key ICT and literacy skills of exploration, publication and communication.

Martin Tibbetts |

NLS: scope and sequence chart

NLS Framework requirements	*Password English* units
WORD LEVEL **Spelling and vocabulary** *Term 1* 2 Identify mis-spelt words; keep lists and learn 3 Use independent spelling strategies 4 Practice spelling with 'look, say, cover, write, check' 5 Two-syllable words with double consonants 6 Common homophones 7 Regular verb endings 8 Irregular tense changes 9 Suffixes 11 Define familiar vocabulary 12 Use 3rd/4th letters to locate/sequence 13 Use rhyming dictionary 14 Change nouns/adjectives into verbs	Spelling strategies 1 Spelling strategies 2,3; Dictionaries 1,2 Spelling strategies 1 Spelling revision 1 Sounds 1 Verb spellings 1 Verb spellings 2 Word endings 1 Word puzzles 3 Word puzzles 2 Word puzzles 1 Transforming words 2
Term 2 2 Identify mis-spelt words; keep lists and learn 3 Use independent spelling strategies 4 Practice spelling with 'look, say, cover, write, check' 5 Suffixes and words ending in *f* 6 Words with common endings 7 Prefixes 9 Alternative words and expressions 10 Words that imply gender 11 Vocabulary changes over time 12 Define familiar words 13 Change nouns/verbs into adjectives	Spelling strategies 1 Spelling strategies 2,3; Dictionaries 1,2 Spelling strategies 1 Word endings 2 Spelling strategies 3 Spelling revision 2 New words 1 Transforming words 1 New words 2 Word puzzles 3 Transforming words 2
Term 3 2 Identify mis-spelt words; keep lists and learn 3 Use independent spelling strategies 4 Practice spelling with 'look, say, cover, write, check' 5 Explore occurrence of letters and letter strings 6 Common roots, different sounds 7 Words with common roots 8 Extending and compounding words 9 Suffixes 10 Forms: *its* and *it's* 11 Compound words 12 Diminutives	Spelling strategies 1 Spelling strategies 2,3; Dictionaries 1,2 Spelling strategies 1 Spelling strategies 2 Sounds 2 Spelling strategies 3 Word endings 2 Word endings 1 Spelling revision 3 Compound words Transforming words 3

NLS Framework requirements	*Password English* units
SENTENCE LEVEL *Grammar and punctuation* *Term 1* 1 Re-read own writing for sense/accuracy 2 Revise verbs and investigate verb tenses 3 Identify use of 'powerful' verbs 4 Adverbs 5 Using commas in sentences	Grammar revision 1 Parts of speech 1,2; Verbs 1,2,3 Verbs 4 Adverbs 1,2 Commas in sentences 1,2
Term 2 1 Revise adjectives, link to stories, poems 2 Use apostrophe for possession 3 Understand word order 4 Commas, connectives and full stops	Parts of speech 1,2; Adjectives 1,2,3 Apostrophes Sentences 1 Sentences 2; Commas in sentences 2
Term 3 1 Changing words 2 Identify and use common punctuation marks 3 Changing sentences 4 Use of connectives in an argument	Grammar revision 2 Punctuation marks 2 Sentences 3 Sentences 2

NLS: scope and sequence chart

NLS Framework requirements	*Password English* units
TEXT LEVEL	
Fiction and poetry	
Term 1	
1 Settings, characters from details	Characters 1; Settings 1
2 Main characteristics of key characters	Characters 2,3
3 Chronology in narrative	Structure and sequence 1
4 Narrative order	Structure and sequence 1,2
5 Prepare, read, perform playscripts	Playscripts 1,3
6 Build-up of play scene	Playscripts 2
7 Compare/contrast poems on similar themes	Common themes in poetry 1,2
8 Popular authors, poets, etc	Authors 1
9/10 Planning stories	Structure and sequence 3
11 Write character sketches	Characters 2
12 Link own experience with historical story	Structure and sequence 4
13 Write playscripts	Playscripts 3
14 Write poems	Common themes in poetry 3
15 Use paragraphs in writing	Structure and sequence 4
Term 2	
1 Investigating imaginary worlds	Settings 1
2 How settings influence events and characters	Settings 2
3 Compare and contrast settings	Settings 2
4 Expressive and descriptive language	Settings 3; Classic and modern poetry 1;
5 Figurative language	Classic and modern poetry 1
6 Clues that suggest older poems	Classic and modern poetry 2
7 Patterns of rhyme and verse in poems	Classic and modern poetry 3
8 Review a range of stories	Authors 2
9 How texts are targeted at readers	Settings 1
10 Use settings in writing	Settings 4
11 Write poems based on those read	Classic/modern poetry 3
12 Collaborate to write in chapters	Settings 4
13 Write descriptive, expressive language	Settings 4
14 Note-making and editing	Settings 4
Term 3	
1 Social, moral, cultural issues in stories	Issues 1
2 Read stories from other cultures	Stories from other cultures 1,2,3
3 Understand paragraphs and chapters	Issues 3
4 Understand poetry terms	Poetry: range of forms 1
5 Clap and count syllables in lines of poetry	Poetry: range of forms 1
6 Explore poets' use of rhyme	Poetry: range of forms 1,2
7 Recognise simple forms of poetry and use	Poetry: range of forms 1,2
8 Write critically about an issue	Issues 2
9 Identify and compare authors' work	Authors 2,3
10 Describe/review own reading habits	Authors 3
11 Write story about dilemma, issues	Issues 4
12 Write alternative ending to known story	Issues 3
13 Write longer stories in chapters from plans	Issues 4
14 Write poems of different styles/structures	Poetry: range of forms 1,2
15 Revise and 'polish' poetry	Poetry: range of forms 4

NLS Framework requirements	*Password English* units
TEXT LEVEL **Non-fiction** *Term 1* 16 Identify different text types 17 Identify features of non-fiction texts 18 Opening sentences and key phrases 19 Understand/use terms *fact* and *opinion* 20 Main features of newspapers 21 Predict newspaper stories from headlines 22 Features of instructional texts 23 Reading strategies and IT texts 24 Write newspaper reports 25 Write clear instructions 26 Improve cohesion of written instructions 27 Write non-chronological report	Newspapers 1 Newspapers 1 Newspapers 3 Newspapers 2 Newspapers 1 Newspapers 3 Instructions 1 Using ICT 1 Newspapers 4 Instructions 2 Instructions 2 Using ICT 2
Term 2 15 Appraise non-fiction book 16 Prepare for factual research 17 Scan texts for key words/phrases 18 Mark extracts by annotation/noting 19 Explore how and why paragraphs are used 20 Identify key features of explanatory texts 21 Make short notes 22 Fill out brief notes into connected prose 23 Present info from sources in simple format 24 Write explanations using linking devices 25 Write explanations of process	Information books 1 Information books 1 Presentation of info 3; Info books 2, 3 Information books 2, 3 Presentation of info 3; Info books 3 Presentation of info 2 Information books 2, 3 Information books 2 Information books 2 Presentation of info 2,4 Presentation of info 2,4
Term 3 16 Read and compare written discussions 17 How arguments are presented 18 Investigate style/vocab of persuasive writing 19 Evaluate advertisements 20 Summarise sentence or paragraph 21 Assemble points to present point of view 22 Use writing frames to back up points of view 23 Present point of view in writing 24 Summarise key ideas in writing 25 Design an advertisement	Discursive writing 1 Discursive writing 2 Persuasive writing 1 Persuasive writing 2 Discursive writing 3 Discursive writing 4 Discursive writing 4 Discursive writing 4 Discursive writing 3 Persuasive writing 3

Source: The National Literacy Strategy: framework for teaching (DfEE, 1998)

Curriculum links: England and Wales

Curriculum requirements	*Password English* coverage
READING	
1. Range	
a. Read a range of literature, progressively more demanding	Text-level fiction and poetry units
b. Read information from range of sources, e.g. IT, encyclopaedias, etc.	Text-level non-fiction units
c. Materials read include number of challenging features	Text-level units
d. Literature covers range of categories	Text-level fiction and poetry units
2. Key Skills	
a. Read with fluency, accuracy, understanding and enjoyment	Text-level units
b. Respond in detail to quality and evaluate texts they read	Text-level fiction and poetry units
c. Find information in books and IT sources	Text-level non-fiction units
d. Use library systems, catalogues and indexes	Text-level units
3. Standard English/Language Study	
Characteristics of different kinds of texts	Text-level units
WRITING	
1. Range	
a. Write for varied purposes	Text-level units
b. Opportunities to write for range of readers and stimuli	Text-level units
c. Use characteristics of different types of writing	Text-level units
2. Key skills	
a. Write in response to more demanding tasks for range of purposes	Text-level units

Curriculum requirements	*Password English* coverage
b. Plan, draft and improve their writing	Text-level units
c. Punctuate writing correctly	Sentence-level punctuation units
d. Spell words correctly, develop vocabulary, using various strategies	Word-level units
3. Standard English/Language Study	
a. Reflect on use of language	General to all units
b. Develop grammar of complex sentences, using standard written forms	Sentence-level grammar units
c. Distinguish words of similar meaning, explain meanings and choose vocabulary	Word-level vocabulary units
SPEAKING AND LISTENING	
1. Range	
a. Opportunities to talk for range of purposes	Whole-class/group sessions
b. Opportunities to communicate to different audiences	Whole-class/group sessions
c. Listen and respond to range of people	Whole-class/group sessions
d. Participate in range of drama activities	*Playscripts*
2. Key Skills	
a. Express themselves confidently and clearly in various contexts	Whole-class/group sessions
b. Listen carefully, identify key features and respond	Text-level units
3. Standard English/Language Study	
a. Develop use of standard English through formal/informal activities	All units
b. Use increasingly varied vocabulary	Word- and sentence-level units

Source: *The National Curriculum (DfEE, 1995)*

Curriculum links: Scotland

Curriculum requirements	*Password English* coverage
READING	
Reading for information Levels C, D	Text-level non-fiction units
Reading for enjoyment Levels C, D	Text-level fiction units
Reading to reflect on the writers' ideas and craft Levels C, D	Text-level units
Awareness of genre (type of text) Levels C, D	Text-level units
Reading aloud Levels C, D	Playscripts
Knowledge about language Levels C, D	All units
WRITING	
Functional writing Levels C, D	Text-level units
Personal writing Levels C, D	Text-level units
Imaginative writing Levels C, D	Text-level fiction units
Punctuation and structure Levels C, D	Sentence-level punctuation units
Spelling Levels C, D	Word-level spelling units
Knowledge about language Levels C, D	Word- and sentence-level units

Curriculum requirements	*Password English* coverage
LISTENING/WATCHING	
Listening for information, instructions and directions Levels C, D	Whole-class/group sessions
Listening in groups Levels C, D	Group sessions
Listening to respond to texts Levels C, D	Text-level units
Awareness of genre (type of text) Levels C, D	Text-level units
Knowledge about language Levels C, D	*Playscripts;* poetry units; non-fiction units
TALKING	
Conveying information, instructions, and directions Levels C, D	Whole-class/group sessions
Talking in groups Levels C, D	Group sessions
Talking about experiences, feelings and opinions Levels C, D	Text-level units
Talking about texts Levels C, D	Text-level units
Audience awareness Levels C, D	Whole-class/group sessions
Knowledge about language Levels C, D	Whole-class/group sessions

Source: *Guidelines on English Language 5-14 (SOED, 1991)*

Curriculum links: Northern Ireland

Curriculum requirements	*Password English* coverage
READING	
Progression	Level 3
Contribution to cross-curricular themes	Scope for cross-curricular and ICT opportunities throughout
Context	Opportunities for reading in different contexts throughout
Range	Text-level units
Purpose	Text-level units
Audience	Text-level units
Reading Activities	Text-level units
Expected outcomes	Text-level units
WRITING	
Progression	Level 3
Contribution to cross-curricular themes	Scope for cross-curricular and ICT opportunities throughout
Planning	Text-level units
Purpose	Text-level units

Curriculum requirements	*Password English* coverage
Context	Text-level units
Audience	Text-level units
Range	Text-level units
Expected outcomes	All units
TALKING AND LISTENING	
Progression	Level 3
Contribution to cross-curricular skills	Scope for cross-curricular and ICT opportunities throughout
Context	Whole-class/group sessions
Audience	Whole-class/group sessions
Purpose	Whole-class/group sessions
Talking and listening activities	Text-level units
Expected outcomes	Whole-class/group sessions

Source: *Northern Ireland Curriculum (DENI, 1996)*

Assessment

Introduction

Teachers using *Password English* will be already using a variety of assessment measures. Some will be undertaking statutory testing at the end of the key stages and increasingly interim assessment materials are being developed for use in other years. Many schools also undertake other forms of assessment and have developed effective approaches to moderating judgements and recording achievement.

This background and expertise is recognised and has influenced the flexible approach to assessment and record-keeping taken in *Password English*. Teachers are invited to make use of their existing assessment arrangements, or to adopt one of the approaches taken here.

Learning objectives

Each *Password English* session identifies specific learning objectives that are addressed through the teaching guidance, development activities and the plenary discussion. These relate closely to the areas for development identified in the programmes of study and in the framework for teaching of the National Literacy Strategy. They are intended both to shape the lesson and to influence the sorts of language the teacher uses to introduce and reinforce the key points. For example, in the session on speech marks, the learning objectives identified are:
- *to identify speech marks and begin to use them in their own writing*
- *to understand and use the term speech marks.*

Such objectives not only influence the kinds of activities described in the unit, but also should be at the forefront of the teacher's thinking throughout the session. In that way, opportunities that arise to extend children's understanding will not be missed and the concluding plenary will be focused closely upon what it was intended for the children to learn. By identifying specific learning objectives in this way, *Password English* is signalling precisely that it is the children's learning, not simply their activity, that is at the heart of each session.

Assessment points

Within each unit, points for assessment are also identified. These statements are closely related to the learning objectives and indicate what the children should be able to do, or what they should know, after completing the session. The assessment points are intended to be immediately recognisable and (if necessary) testable. A teacher might use these assessment points to test the understanding of all or some of the children in the class at the end of the unit of work, or some time later, as a means of assessing the security of the knowledge or skill. The differentiated activities provided in the unit inevitably mean that children will have approached the topic in different ways and their understanding is also variable; teachers will want to make a judgement about how far they have achieved the specific target and plan subsequent teaching accordingly.

The assessment points identified represent small steps of knowledge, skill or understanding within the areas of the curriculum being addressed. Various methods of plotting progress and assessment are provided on the following pages on photocopiable sheets.

Assessment

Assessment criteria

It should be remembered, however, that summative judgements about performance and the standard of work at the end of each year or key stage should properly be made against nationally-agreed criteria, such as level descriptions.

Assessment formats

Two principal assessment formats are provided. Assessment sheet 1 is intended to help you keep track of interesting developments observed, moments of insight expressed orally by children, or to record your own observations about the children's work in the different activities. This informal recording format might be left on your desk during the lesson, available to capture both children's thoughts and comments and your own response to the activity. Here you might perhaps identify follow-up activities that suggest themselves or areas of weakness that might be addressed by providing specific exercises or activities.

Assessment sheet 2 is intended for post-lesson reflection on the work achieved by different children. It could be attached to particularly significant pieces of work, which demonstrate a significant move forward for the child in a particular area of the curriculum, are particularly illustrative of the achievement of particular assessment criteria, or demonstrate a specific weakness or area for development.

In addition to these recording formats, you are also provided with a number of tables which allow you to map the path that individual children take through the course, marking which activities were undertaken by which children. This should be useful in deciding on subsequent or reinforcement activities.

Notes on assessment sheets	*Note: each of the sheets are photocopiable and should be enlarged to A4 size for ease of use. You may find it necessary to adapt these sheets and produce versions tailored to your specific needs.*
Sheet 1	**Session commentary** This sheet could be used to record significant elements of children's work (e.g. attitudes, difficulties, questions, evidence of understanding) and your own observations of the success of the activity, follow up, and areas to investigate further.
Sheet 2	**Recording evidence** This sheet could be used to attach to individual pieces of work that are particularly significant, perhaps because they represent a major step forward for the individual child, they are representative of work at a particular level or illuminate assessment criteria well, or they indicate a particular need that should be addressed urgently.
Sheet 3	**Achievement – summary** This sheet could be used to record individual, class or group achievement against selected learning objectives (for up to five sessions). The boxes could be used to simply tick areas of achievement, or to write brief notes.
Sheet 4	**Achievement – detail** This sheet is a detailed version of sheet 3 that could be used to record achievement in a single session.
Sheet 5	**Class skills coverage grid** This grid could be used to keep track of the course coverage for each child in the class. Enter the names of your class across the top of the grid. In the left-hand column is space to list each of the assessment points within the session. Mark the achievement of the children in each session.

Assessment 1: Session commentary

Session:	Learning objectives:
Class/year group:	

Focus here on children's attitudes, difficulties, questions, comments, evidence of understanding.	*Focus here on your own observations about the success of the activity, points to follow up, areas to investigate further.*
Whole-class introduction and activity	
Activity 1	
Activity 2	
Activity 3	
Activity 4	
Activity 5	
Plenary	

Assessment 2: Recording evidence

Name:	Title of piece of work:
Year: Age:	Date:

Context in which the work was completed
(Indicate whether this was undertaken individually or in a group, whether the work is a first draft or has been revised, note the degree of support, etc.)

Significant features noted about this piece of work

How does this compare with the child's previous work, my expectations, national assessment criteria?

What action should I take?
❏ *Add the work and annotation to the child's individual record*
❏ *Add it to the school's assessment portfolio*
❏ *Discuss this with the child and/or parents*
❏ *Discuss this with colleagues, the English co-ordinator, the Headteacher*

Ensure that this is followed up by:

Additional notes

Assessment 3: Achievement – summary

Name/Group/Class:
....

	Activity attempted	Basic grasp of concept	Sound grasp of concept	**Support, practice, extension**

Session title:

Assessment point 1				
Assessment point 2				
Date/additional information				

Session title:

Assessment point 1				
Assessment point 2				
Date/additional information				

Session title:

Assessment point 1				
Assessment point 2				
Date/additional information				

Session title:

Assessment point 1				
Assessment point 2				
Date/additional information				

Session title:

Assessment point 1				
Assessment point 2				
Date/additional information				

Assessment 4: Achievement – detail

Name/Group/Class: ....

Session title:	Assessment point 1	Assessment point 2

Activity attempted		
Basic grasp of concept		
Sound grasp of concept		

Support, practice, extension		

Date/additional information		

Assessment 5: Class skills coverage grid

Session title:

| Assessment point 1 |
| Assessment point 2 |

Session title:

| Assessment point 1 |
| Assessment point 2 |

Session title:

| Assessment point 1 |
| Assessment point 2 |

Session title:

| Assessment point 1 |
| Assessment point 2 |

Simmering activities

Introduction

The activities in this section are designed to provide ongoing practice of a range of key literacy skills at word, sentence and text level. They are intended to be short, snappy, fun activities that could be used outside the literacy hour in 'spare' time, such as:
- first thing in the morning
- between lessons
- before play
- before going home
- before assembly.

These activities are not intended to be comprehensive – they are merely a range of ideas to keep literacy concepts 'on the go' and provide informal practice. No doubt you will know many similar activities and games that will keep concepts alive in the children's minds.

The activities are readily adaptable for use with individuals, groups or the whole class, depending on the needs of the children.

Contents

Word level
Spelling   244
Vocabulary   246
Sentence level
Grammar   248
Punctuation   250
Text level
Fiction and poetry   252
Non-fiction   254

Simmering activities

WORD level	SPELLING
Spelling strategies	**Spot the spelling mistake:** write six words on separate flash cards: three words should be mis-spelt. Reveal each word for ten seconds. Which ones are wrong? Talk about the importance of checking critical features: does the word look right? Is it the right length/shape?
Sounds	**Rogue words:** prepare some flash cards of words of similar sounds, and include 'rogue' words of similar spelling but different sounds, e.g. *eight, fate, height, straight; least, feat, meat, break,* etc. Hold them up one at a time for whole class to read aloud. Speed up the switching of cards and try and catch the class out. **Homophone challenge:** use a dictionary to find and list as many homophone pairs as possible in a set time. (Try this with homophone trios – much more difficult!)
Verb spellings	**Verb lists:** compile lists of as many verbs as possible in two minutes, each with the ending *-ing* (or alternatively *-ed, -s*). ***Dictation:*** dictate a short text from a known reading book as a spelling test, focusing on common irregular past-tense verbs, e.g. *went, sat, ran*.
Word endings	**Plural spelling test:** write the following words in plural: *elf, robin, giraffe, leaf, belief, rabbit, thief, robber, half* and *quarter*. Mark the test in pairs.

	Exceptions: work in pairs to list as many words as possible that are exceptions to a given rule, e.g. adding suffixes to words ending in *-f* or *-fe* (e.g. *roofs*).
Compound words	**Quickfire compound words:** say a word to each child, and they should reply with a compound word containing that word, e.g. *run, fast, fire, room, fall, post, clock, bow, sun, air.*
	Beat the clock: in a given time, write as many compound words as possible. Include nonsense words if necessary, then sort them out!
Spelling revision	**Prefix sprint:** write 20 words with prefixes. When a child reaches 20 and calls out 'finished', stop the class and go through their answers. As they become more proficient, increase the target number of prefixes.
	Double trouble: as a whole class, list on the board as many two-syllable words with double consonants as possible. How many of them have an alternative single-consonant form, e.g. *dinner-diner*?
	Contraction game: in groups, list as many contracted forms as possible in one minute, e.g. *don't, can't*. Then pass the list to the next group: on the word 'go' the group must write every contracted word in its uncontracted form (e.g. *don't = do not*). The game stops when one group completes its list of uncontracted words, and is the winner.

Simmering activities

WORD level	VOCABULARY
Dictionaries	**Beat the dictionary:** give one child (the adjudicator) a dictionary, and ask everyone in the class to write or memorise the most difficult word they can think of. Then pick out a child to say his or her word. Ask the rest of the class to volunteer suggestions of its meaning, and then ask the adjudicator to read out the definition. Are there any words that baffle the whole class?
Word puzzles	**Make a word:** write nine randomly-chosen letters on the board, including between five and seven consonants. The children write down as many words as they can using these letters in three minutes. At the end, find out who has the most words. What is the longest word found?
	Alphabetical queues: ask the children to organise themselves into reverse alphabetical order by surname in a set time, when queuing (e.g. for lunch).
	Definitions: write up five common words and ask the children to define each word in a given number of words, e.g. *define 'tree' in three words.*
New words	**Word association:** one child says a word, e.g. *sky*, and the next comes up with a related word (e.g. *blue*), and the next with another word, and so on. If anybody hesitates or gives a non-related word and is challenged by another child, they are excluded from the game. To make things a little harder, tell the children they cannot use words already used in the game.

Word disassociation: similar to *Word association*, except each child must produce a word unrelated to the previous word (e.g. *dog – starfish*). This is more difficult than it sounds – the children could challenge and relate seemingly unrelated words (e.g. *dog* and *starfish* are both animals)!

Word association with hot words: again, similar to *Word association*, except children gain bonus points by saying 'hot words' (e.g. recently learned words you might want to reinforce the sound and meaning of). Each 'hot word' must be related to the previous word.

Butterfly game: write up a starter word, e.g. *butterfly*, and then ask the children to write the longest related words they can think of (e.g. *caterpillar, cocoon*, etc) in one minute. Ask them to volunteer their words and discuss the meanings of the words they come up with.

Transforming words

Adjectives race: in two minutes, list as many nouns as possible that can be transformed into adjectives (e.g. *dread, colour, beauty*, etc). Pass the list to the next group, so that all groups have another group's list. On the command 'go', the group must transform all the nouns into adjectives as quickly as possible, and on completing the list, shout 'stop'. Go through the answers and adjudicate.

Diminutive race: in two minutes, brainstorm as many diminutives as possible, including proper nouns. Which are 'real' diminutives?

Simmering activities

SENTENCE level	GRAMMAR
Parts of speech	**Noun-adjective-verb:** ask a child to think of a noun; ask the next child to think of an adjective that begins with the last letter of the noun; then a verb, then a noun and so on, e.g. *car, red, dare*.
Verbs	**Verb count:** read a story and ask the children to write every verb they hear. At the end of the story, each child counts up their verbs. Find the child with the highest score and check all his or her verbs are correct. (This could also be done with adjectives or adverbs.)
	Change the tense: one child names a verb, the next has to use it in past tense, and the third in future tense. The next child then names a new verb, and so on (e.g. *make-I will make-I made*) around the class.
	Just a minute: each child has to talk about a favourite topic or activity to their group for as long as possible, using just one tense. The others call 'stop' if another tense is used. The next child then begins to talk in a different tense, and so on. The winner is the child who keeps this up the longest.
Adverbs	**Adverb brainstorm:** give the children an action – e.g. *the rabbit ran, the monster roared, the bird sang*, and brainstorm suitable adverbs. Try again with a new action, and so on. Introduce own suggestions and new adverbs if necessary.

Guess the adverb: someone mimes an action performed in a particular way (e.g. shutting a door quietly); the others try to guess the adverb.

Adjectives

Adjective chain: one child says a noun, then the next says an adjective that describes it. The next child says another noun that the adjective might describe, and then the next child an adjective to describe that noun and so on (e.g. *elephant – large – whale – blue*). Continue around the class.

Adjective chase: show the children a picture, e.g. a dinosaur or a flower garden. The children in groups must come up with a list of as many appropriate adjectives as they can in just two minutes. The winner is the group with the most suitable adjectives. If an unsuitable adjective is given, children must appeal by sticking their hands in the air. After a short discussion, hold a class vote to decide whether the adjective can be used or not.

Sentences

What's the question?: in groups, one child thinks of an answer, and the next has to say the question that goes with the answer. This continues until somebody produces a wrong question or can't think of an answer and drops out.

Make a sentence: in groups, one child starts a sentence '*Barney*', then the next child says the next word, and so on. End it (correctly) by saying, e.g. *full stop* (e.g. *Barney-hit-the-dog-and-it-ran-away-full stop*).

Simmering activities

SENTENCE level	PUNCTUATION
Commas in sentences	**List sentence game:** write up the first half of a sentence on the board, e.g. *At the zoo I saw … .* The first child adds a suitable word, e.g. *At the zoo I saw a tiger*, then the next child repeats the whole sentence adding a new animal, and so on, e.g. the fifth child might say *At the zoo I saw a tiger, rhino, gazelle, lion and a bear.* **Spot the comma:** read an extract from a known reading book, and ask the children to call out *comma* whenever they think you have reached a comma in the text. (This could be extended to other punctuation.) **Comma quiz:** write up a selection of short sentences with the commas missing, and ask the children to insert them. Then ask the children to come up with some sample sentences themselves, for the rest of the class to work out.
Apostrophes	**Apostrophe test:** challenge the children to spell a range of nouns, all with possessive apostrophes, e.g. singular nouns (*man's, cat's, car's, school's, girl's*), regular plural nouns (*horses', doctors', trees', boys', birds'*) and irregular plural nouns (*children's, men's, cattle's, sheep's, geese's*). **Apostrophe see-saw:** one child comes up with a sentence containing an apostrophe for possession, the next child comes up with a sentence containing an apostrophe for contraction, and so on around the class.

Punctuation marks

Adding punctuation: write up three or four sentences on the board, including some dialogue, without any punctuation. Ask the children to suggest where punctuation marks should go.

Punctuation train: one child starts a sentence, e.g. *Doctor Foster went to Gloucester – comma* (or full stop, or other suitable punctuation), and the next child has to continue, correctly taking into account the punctuation, e.g. *a town in western England – full stop*. Carry on like this (either orally or in writing) until a child makes an error.

Spot the capital: read from a story or information book, preferably with lots of capital letters in the text, and ask the children to say *capital* every time you read a capitalised word.

Punctuation puzzler: read to the children from a known story book, but ignore all the punctuation. Then read the same extract again (slowly) and ask the children to suggest which punctuation marks go where in the text.

Dictation: read a short text to the children that includes more complex punctuation, e.g. hyphens, dashes, colons. The children should write the text and pay particular attention to the position of the punctuation.

Descriptions: describe punctuation marks in detail and ask the children to guess each one, e.g. *like two tadpoles up in the air (speech marks)*.

Simmering activities

TEXT level	FICTION AND POETRY
Authors	**Author discussion:** give an author name (and if possible, a copy of one of their books) to each group. Choose books the children will be familiar with. Each child writes reasons why they like or dislike this author's books in two minutes. They then each read out their reasons, and a group vote is held on whether they like the author or not.
Playscripts	**Mini-play:** give each group a title, e.g. *Lost in the jungle*, *Alien encounter*, and ask them to write the first few lines of dialogue. Then ask each group to perform a quick role-play.
Characters	**Lost in a lifeboat:** allocate each group the same scene, *adrift in a lifeboat*, and problem, *the food and water has run out*. For three minutes children have to ad-lib this situation, taking on whatever role they feel like, or being themselves. Then as a whole class, discuss who made helpful suggestions, who was gloomy, who said very little and who was unhelpful, etc. Finish by pointing out and discussing the different characters. **Strange characters:** in each mixed-ability group, give each child one feature of a character to make up, e.g. name, appearance, clothes worn, what he or she does, where he or she is from, or what he or she owns. Each child writes 'their' feature secretly and then after two minutes one person from the group collects all the features together and reads out the 'group character'.

Structure and sequence	**Making up a story:** give the class an introductory sentence, e.g. *The big unsinkable ship set sail for America.; A huge dragon was terrorising the small kingdom.;* etc. Brainstorm the next part of the story, and write up the best suggestions on the board. Then brainstorm a conclusion and discuss the suggestions.
Settings	**Strange settings:** allocate each group a setting, e.g. *strange planet, haunted house, fairy tale forest, spaceship, desert island.* They have two minutes to make up, discuss and write down five unusual things about the setting.
Stories from other cultures	**What's my country?:** ask a group to pretend they have woken up in a different country (which they know something about) by accident, and the rest of the class have to guess where it is by asking them questions – they can reply only *yes/no/don't know.*
Classic and modern poetry	**Poem of the week:** each group in turn chooses a 'poem of the week' and presents ideas about why they like it, the ideas and images it contains, etc.
Poetry: range of forms	**Haiku challenge:** individually or in groups, write a haiku about a chosen subject in a set time. Who can write the most creative and effective haiku? **Limerick lunacy:** give the class the first line of a limerick and complete it together.

Simmering activities

TEXT level	NON-FICTION
Newspapers	**Headlines game:** read out these imaginary newspaper headlines, one at a time. Ask the children to discuss in their groups what they could be about. *Hurricane hits Florida - thousands in danger; Top band split up – fans distressed; Poor night for Britain at Oscars; Gap at top of Premiership narrows.* **Write the headlines:** use short stories from a local newspaper, with the headlines removed or masked, and ask the children to write new headlines and/or opening sentences.
Instructions	**Instruction challenge:** one group at a time reads out a set of simple instructions, e.g. *using a word-processor*, without explaining what they are for. The first group from the rest of the class to guess what the instructions are about is the winner!
Presentation of information	**Good and bad:** using class texts, find one example of good presentation, and one example of bad presentation. Present the examples to the rest of the class. Which are the best and worst of all?
Information books	**Present a book:** each group chooses an information book they have found especially useful in recent work, and presents it to the rest of the class with an explanation of why they have found it so useful.

Persuasive writing	**The hard sell game:** allocate each group a product, e.g. a fizzy drink, a computer game, an action doll, training shoes, an airline, etc. The group has to come up with five good things about this product (which can be made up) in two minutes, and one child reads these to the rest of the class. Each person in the class outside the group votes on whether they would buy the product.

Advertisement challenge: each group writes a 30-second radio or television advertisement for something at school they dislike, e.g. spelling tests, school dinners. Even though they dislike it, they must try hard to persuade others that it is a good thing! Each group presents their advertisement in turn.

Find the ad: in a set time (e.g. two minutes), use the class collection of newspapers and magazines to find as many advertisements for a chosen product as possible, e.g. washing powder. |
| *Discursive writing* | **Class discussion:** choose an issue to discuss as a class or a group, e.g. a local issue, a school event, etc. Spend a short time preparing points for or against the issue, then hold a discussion – either as a whole class, or in groups.

Television debate: choose a well-known television programme and write a list of points 'for' and 'against' watching it. Hold a class vote on whether the programme is good or bad. |

Notes